100 bright ideas for
YOUR HOME

Tamsin Weston

100 bright ideas for
YOUR HOME

BETTERWAY BOOKS
Cincinnati, Ohio

First published in North America in 2002 by

Betterway Books,

 an imprint of F&W Publications, Inc.,

4700 East Galbraith Road

Cincinnati, OH 45236

1-800-289-0963

ISBN 1-55870-631-3

A CIP catalogue record for this book is available from the British Library

Printed and bound in China

10 9 8 7 6 5 4 3 2 1

Contents

Introduction

Choosing furnishings in the form of upholstery, loose covers, cushions, throws, curtains and blinds can be the most exciting part of putting a room scheme together. There is a such a vast array of different patterns and colour combinations that it is a good idea to make your own 'mood board' with swatches and colours that you like. Collect pictures from magazines of rooms that you like too. This will help you to get an idea of what colours and patterns work together before rushing in.

Bright ideas
Each chapter in this book is divided into the following four sections.

DONE IN A DAY
Projects requiring some basic DIY skills that you will be able to complete in a day or less.

 ### QUICK FIX
Instant ideas which are simple to follow and will take less than a morning.

GOOD IDEAS
A gallery of inspirations for good buys and finishing touches to make a difference quickly.

GET THE LOOK
Whole decorating schemes for you to recreate and adapt to your own style, with tips on how to achieve the look.

Key to symbols used in this book
Check how long the project will take and how easy it is to do with the at-a-glance guide.

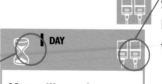

 SKILL LEVEL Tells you how easy or difficult the project is.

HOW LONG Tells you how long the project will take.

You will need
- tape measure
- fabric
- sewing machine or needle and cotton

easy

medium

difficult

Colour themes

There are endless options and varieties of colour combinations to choose from. This book is divided into five of the most popular decorating combinations around today – classic combinations, new naturals, fresh florals, pretty pastels and bold brights. You will find most soft furnishing manufacturers will have a particular pattern in a whole selection of colourways, from bright and bold down to neutral mixes and muted, paler combinations.

If you are planning your room scheme from scratch, rather than using a patterned fabric or wallcovering as a base, start by choosing a main colour – this is the colour that there will be most of. Next choose a secondary colour which will be used in roughly half the amount of the main colour; and a third, accent, colour to add in smaller proportions, such as cushions, trimmings and accessories.

Choosing fabrics

It is important to choose carefully the fabrics you are planning to use, considering the proportions of the design and the colour in relation to your room scheme. The scale of the fabric design should also be related to the size and the shape of the piece to be furnished. For example, choose a relatively narrow stripe to upholster a small piece of furniture and wider stripes for a larger piece. Think about how much fabric you will need and the areas you are covering – do you need plain

Above left: Citrus colours, such as lemon yellow, orange and lime work wonderfully together to create a vibrant, zingy style.

Above right: Have fun with fabrics by using two or three different designs in the same colourway. Here, florals and checks create a charming look.

coordinating fabric to work with a pattern to make the scheme easier to live with? You may already have a large expanse of patterned or coloured fabric that you want to use as a basis for your scheme – in which case you have to think about smaller elements of colour and pattern to add to the room.

Combining different patterns together can add variety and colour. For instance, you may have a floral theme in a bedroom, but checks or stripes can work wonderfully with this if you choose the right colours and proportions. If you find this part of decorating a little overwhelming, stick to just three colours and you can't go wrong.

Practical considerations

Don't forget practical aspects, especially when it comes to wear and tear; there are important considerations and questions you need to ask yourself. For example, what will the room be used for? Who will be using it? Are there children using the room? The answers will help you to make some of the more practical decisions. Loose covers that can be put in the washing machine are a good option if you have young children or lively teenagers. Stain-protection finishes are another option, but make sure they conform to fire regulations. Perhaps the most important practical consideration, however, is that the furniture you choose needs to be comfortable, especially if it will get a lot of use.

1 **Classic combinations:** simple and effective, blue and white fabrics work brilliantly together and suit many styles of decor.

2 **New naturals:** soft furnishings in neutral tones are easy to live with and will work in any room. Creamy, natural shades have softness and warmth while darker tones like coffee and chocolate shades add depth and contrast.

3 **Fresh florals:** there is an enormous range of floral fabrics to choose from and, depending on the design you choose, they can be adapted to fit in with traditional or contemporary room schemes.

4 **Pretty pastels:** the pastel palette is a delight to work with, and you can mix and match a number of different hues without the effect becoming overpowering.

5 **Bold brights:** rich colours bring drama to a room. Although they are most popularly used for dining areas and children's rooms, don't shrink from using them in sitting rooms or bedrooms.

Bedrooms

In the bedroom, bedlinen is normally a dominant player and there is a huge range of different styles, colours and patterns to choose from. Classic colours and styles work best in traditional bedrooms while neutrals, bright colours and bolder prints tend to suit more contemporary settings. Monochrome schemes and pale, muted colours help to create a relaxing atmosphere. Many people choose to decorate their bedroom around a favourite bedlinen set. This is a good way to choose coordinating colours, but don't forget to add accent colours and smaller details.

Finishing touches

You may not want to change your whole room scheme. Sometimes the small touches can make all the difference and make the room complete – even a single chair covered in a new fabric can transform a room. In the living room, the sofa is the most important piece of furniture. A well-dressed sofa can include any array of patterns as long as these coordinate with the overall scheme in the room.

Small details and finishing touches such as cushions, throws, trimmings, lampshades and smaller accessories are an important factor in giving the room a finished feel. Cushion covers and throws provide an easy way to add instant colour and variation to a room without spending a fortune, while trimmings, fringing, tassels and braid can finish pieces off with delicate detail.

Above: Bedlinen can set the tone for the whole bedroom: there is a marvellous choice in the shops, but it's fun to decorate plain linen with your own design.

Above: Small details can make all the difference to a finished look. Consider trimmings, beads and sequins to add an extra special touch.

Tips and techniques

Here is a quick reference guide to some of the materials involved in the projects in this book.

BASIC KIT

These items form a basic set of sewing equipment:

Dressmaking scissors

Tape measure or steel ruler

Iron and ironing board

Pencil

Tailor's chalk/pencil

Pins and needles

Sewing machine

Cottons and threads

SCISSORS

It is important to have a good pair of dressmaking scissors for cutting fabrics. You can now buy both right and left-handed pairs. Scissors range from the small embroidery type to large dressmaking shears. A pair about 20–25cm (8–10in) long should be fine. It may also be helpful to have a small pair of scissors for trimming and clipping.

TAPE MEASURE

It is worth having a good tape measure that extends to about 3m (3¼yds) for curtains, and a smaller soft one for measuring around corners and difficult curves. A ruler is also very useful when you are measuring out a perfect square on fabrics for cushions and other projects that involve square pieces of fabric.

NEEDLES

You may need a selection of sizes, lengths and thicknesses depending on the type of fabrics and cottons you are using.

PINS

Good, sharp pins work in both fine and heavy fabrics. Look out for pins with glass heads as they can be easier to handle and are easily seen in the fabric and they tend not to hurt your fingertips when pushing them into the fabric.

IRON-ON HEM TAPE

This is a great device which can be used as an alternative to sewing hems. You will need to follow the manufacturer's instructions but normally you will need to use a damp sponge to help fix it along with an iron.

EYELET KITS

Eyelet kits can be bought in packs which contain eyelets and the device you need to fix the eyelets on to the fabric. You can find eyelets in a range of sizes and finishes such as silver and gold.

TAILOR'S CHALK

This is a useful way of marking fabrics as it is only temporary and won't stain or mark fabrics permanently. It comes in several forms including flat or pencil shaped.

COTTONS AND THREADS

Matching colours are only really necessary for stitching that will actually show. The advantage of using a cotton thread is that it can be ripped out if you make a mistake, whereas polyester thread will need to be snipped or unpicked because it is so strong that it could tear holes in fabric.

SEWING MACHINES

A sewing machine is the best way to achieve quick and effective results and can save you a great deal of time. It's always a good idea to try out different stitches on scraps of fabric before you start, to make sure the tension is correct. Most sewing machines have a wide range of stitches that you can use so you can be versatile with the effects you want to achieve.

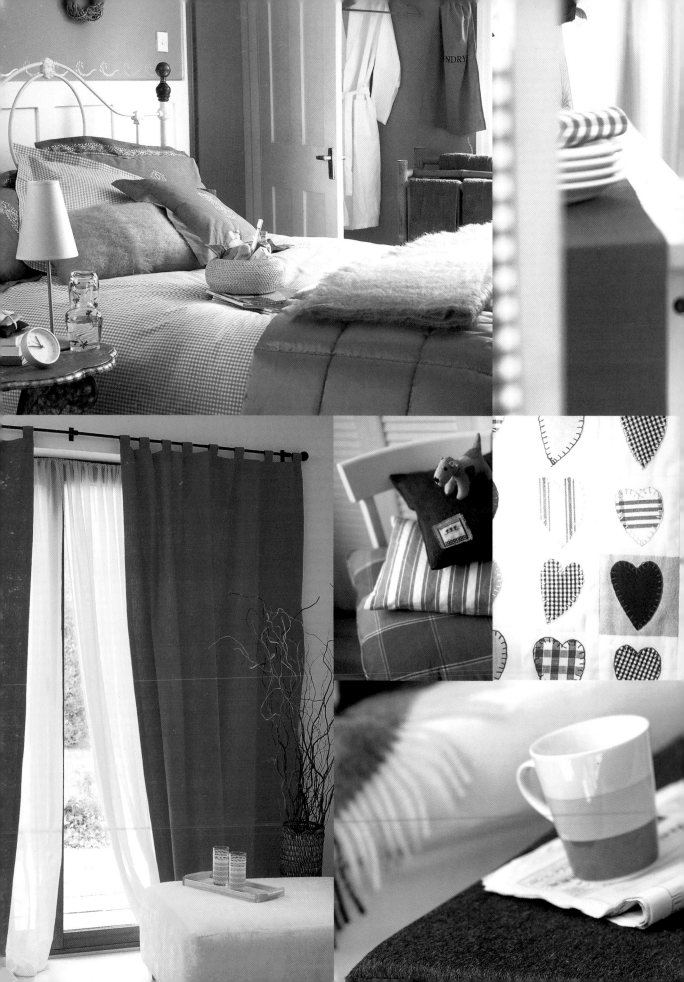

Classic combinations

Classic combinations are timeless and ever-popular schemes that can work in both traditional or contemporary settings, depending on how they are used and the furniture that is used with them. Blue and white creates a fresh look that can work in practically any room, while adding red to this combination gives a completely different feel altogether. Red and white gives a dramatic, bold effect and can look wonderful in dining rooms and kitchens if used in the right proportions. These classic combinations generally include mid tones to create a sharp, clean and crisp look.

Gingham border

Gingham ribbon adds a smart finishing touch to plain
white bedlinen. Use navy blue check for a crisp, clean look.

1 Pin the wider ribbon along all four edges of the sheet, folding it over carefully at the corners. Use a sewing machine to stitch it in place along the inside and outside edges.

2 Cut six lengths of narrow ribbon, each 120cm (48in) long, and set aside two lengths for the pillowcases. Shape four lengths into a figure of eight, following the picture, and secure with pins to each of the four corners of the sheet. Stitch in place along the inside and outside edges.

3 Lay the sheet on a flat surface and mark out the position of the centre border using pins. Position a

⏳ **4 HOURS**

You will need
- about 12.5m (15 yards) of 39mm (1½in) ribbon
- pins
- scissors
- large white sheet
- sewing machine
- about 9m (10½ yards) of 23mm (⅞in) ribbon
- white pillowcases
- iron

length of narrow ribbon on the marked border and pin into place. When you reach each corner, carefully twist the ribbon into a figure of eight, using the picture as a guide, and keeping it as flat as possible. Pin the ribbon then stitch both edges, starting with the outside edge.

4 In the same way, make a figure of eight with the two reserved pieces of narrow ribbon, one on each pillowcase, and pin in place. Stitch the loops on both edges, starting with the outside edge. Iron the ribbon with a warm iron. Add ribbon loops to other accessories for a coordinated look.

American folk wallhanging

Use scraps of gingham, denim and striped fabric to make a patchwork wallhanging in traditional American folk style.

1 Cut out 16 squares, all the same size, from a plain cotton fabric. Pin them together to form one large square and machine stitch the seams.

2 Cut out 16 fabric hearts from a variety of materials and attach one to each square using iron-on hem tape. Use a thick cotton thread to blanket stitch around the outline of each heart for a hand-finished feel.

3 Cut four strips of coordinating fabric to edge the square and pin in place. Cut four squares of gingham ribbon and sew these on to the corners of the strips you have just attached. Now sew the strips on to the square to form a border edging.

4 Cut another four strips from plain coordinating fabric and sew on to the edges of the square for the final border. Cover the backs of the strips with wadding.

5 Cut small lengths of gingham ribbon and sew these to the top side of the back of the wallhanging to form loops. Finally, cover the back of the wallhanging with plain fabric and thread the loops through a dowelling pole to hang it up.

 **4 HOURS**

You will need
- plain fabric in 2 colours
- pencil or tailor's chalk
- scissors
- tape measure
- pins
- sewing machine or needle and cotton
- scraps of patterned fabrics
- iron-on hem tape
- thick cotton thread
- gingham ribbon
- wadding
- dowelling

Garden chair cushions

Use simple tea towels to make a seat cushion and
headrest with handy pocket, for your garden chairs.

2 HOURS per chair

You will need

- 4 large tea towels
- scissors
- tape measure
- pins
- sewing machine or needle and cotton
- iron
- 40x30cm (16x12in) cushion pad
- eight 40cm (16in) lengths of satin ribbon
- 45x45cm (18x18in) cushion pad

1 For the headrest, trim the side seams from two of the tea towels so they are around 44cm (17½in) wide. Lay one tea towel, right side up, on a flat surface. Fold up one short end to form a pocket approximately 23cm (9in) deep. Pin and sew the sides together, allowing a 2cm (¾in) seam. Press the seams open, then turn the fabric to the right side. Repeat with the second tea towel.

2 Lay one headrest piece, pocket side up, on a flat surface. Lay the second, pocket side up, on top. Pin the top edges together and check the fit of the headrest on the chair. If the pockets are hanging down too low, reposition the pins until the fit is just right. Sew the two pieces together with a seam of around 2cm (¾in). Press the seam open and turn to the right side.

3 Insert the smaller cushion pad into the front pocket, then fit the headrest on to the chair. Mark on each pocket where you want to stitch the ribbons and neatly sew a length of ribbon to each side of each pocket. Secure the headrest by tying the ribbons together.

4 To make the seat cushion cover, cut a square, approximately 49x49cm (19½x19½in), from one tea towel. Trim along the long sides of the remaining tea towel to leave a rectangle around 49cm (19½in) wide and cut it in half widthways. Lay the square piece, right side up, on a flat surface. Position the two halves on top, right sides down, so they overlap in the centre with their hemmed edges. Pin all the way around the cushion cover's edges and then machine stitch, allowing a 2cm (¾in) seam.

5 Remove the pins and turn the cover to the right side. Stitch the ribbons, in two pairs, to adjacent corners of the cover. Insert the square cushion pad and fasten to the chair back with the ribbon ties.

Fabric cube

A versatile fabric cube can double as a useful table or comfy seat when guests arrive.

1 Cover the top of the table with wadding, stretching it over the sides and fixing in place under the table top with a staple gun. Wrap a length of wadding all the way around the four sides of the table to form a box and secure in place with staples, as before.

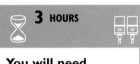

3 HOURS

You will need
- small square table
- wadding
- scissors
- staple gun
- tape measure
- fabric
- pins
- sewing machine or needle and cotton
- iron
- 2cm (¾in) thick foam

2 Measure the top of the table and the four sides. Cut out five pieces of fabric to these measurements, adding an extra 1cm (⅜in) on all sides for hems. Sew together the four pieces of fabric for the sides of the cube, keeping right sides together. Pin the top piece to the side pieces, then sew in place. Turn the cube right sides out and press. Hem around the bottom edges and slip the fabric cover over the table.

3 Measure the top of the cube and cut the foam to fit. Cut out two pieces of fabric to the same measurements, adding an extra 2cm (¾in) on all sides for hems.

4 Sew the pieces of fabric together with a 1cm (⅜in) seam allowance, keeping right sides together and leaving one short end open. Turn right sides out and place the foam inside. Stitch the opening closed. Place the foam on top of the table.

Chair runners

Transform plain dining chairs with simple but elegant
fabric covers that can be echoed in napkins and tablecloths.

1 Measure and cut the
fabric to fit each chair,
allowing the fabric to run
from the floor behind, up
the back of the chair, down
the front of the backrest,
across the seat and down
to the floor in front. Allow
an extra 1cm (⅜in) on all
sides for hems.

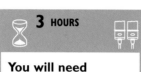

⧖ **3 HOURS**

You will need
• tape measure
• fabric
• pins
• sewing machine or
needle and cotton
• iron
• ribbon

2 Fold over the raw edges, pin and hem, then press the
edges. Place the runners over the chairs.

3 Use a pin to mark the runners at the bottom of the
chair back on both sides as a guide for fixing the ties.

4 Cut two lengths of ribbon for each side of each
runner to act as ties. Put the runners back over the
chairs and pin the ribbon ties to the fabric. These will
need to be placed where the chair back meets the seat.
Sew the ribbons in position and tie around the chair
legs in a bow.

Colourful curtain tops

Create a touch of country style with an easy-to-sew
checked heading that will add interest to plain curtains.

1 Remove any heading
from the curtains, and
resew any open seams.
Wash, dry and press the
heading fabric to make it
easier to sew.

2 Measure and cut the
heading fabric, making it
16cm (6½in) wider than
the curtain, and 10cm (4in) longer than you want the
finished heading to be. Turn under and stitch a 1cm
(⅜in) double hem on one long edge, which will form the
lower edge of the heading. Hem all other edges.

4 HOURS

You will need
- plain curtains
- scissors
- sewing machine or
  needle and cotton
- fabric for heading
- iron
- tape measure
- curtain rings
- curtain clips

3 Lay the heading fabric right side down on a flat
surface with the double hem at the top and lay the
curtain, right side up, on top of it, positioning it
centrally on the width. Overlap the two by 7cm (2¾in).
Stitch across the top of the curtain to secure the two
together (this will be invisible on the finished curtain).

4 Fold the heading over on to the right side of curtain
and wrap the ends around the curtain to the back.
Stitch all the edges in place by hand. Repeat with the
second curtain. Attach the curtain rings to the pole and
the clips to the curtain, then hang them at the window.

Blanket box

Combine a seat with practical storage space to keep your bedroom free of clutter.

1 Measure the box and calculate how much tongue and groove panelling you will need. You can cover the box all round, or just the front and sides. If the widths do not fit exactly trim a plank to fit. Mark the measurements on the tongue and groove planks, then cut to size.

2 Use wood glue to fix the tongue and groove on to the box. When dry, give the entire box a coat of primer and allow to dry. Next apply one or two coats of oil-based paint. Leave to dry.

⏳ **5 HOURS**

You will need
- wooden box with lid
- tape measure
- tongue and groove panelling
- pencil
- saw
- strong wood glue
- wood primer
- paintbrush
- 4cm (1½in) deep foam
- craft knife
- fabric
- sewing machine or needle and cotton
- pins
- touch-and-close tape

3 Cut the foam to fit the lid of the box. Cut a piece of fabric 40cm (16in) wider than the long edges of the cushion and long enough to wrap right round the cushion with an extra 15cm (6in) to spare. Turn under the long edges of the fabric and sew 1.5cm (⅝in) hems. Place the foam in the centre on the wrong side of the fabric. Fold over the long edges so the fabric overlaps in the middle of the foam.

4 Fold over the short edges, mitring the corners exactly as if you were wrapping a present, and pin in place. Remove the foam and handstitch the fabric where it is pinned. Sew touch-and-close tape to the central seam. Replace the foam pad, close the opening with the touch-and-close tape and place the cushion, seams down, on the lid of the box.

Voile and gingham blind

Add a gingham panel to a plain voile blind for a pretty blue and white touch.

1 Cut the voile 2cm (¾in) wider than the window and 18cm (7in) shorter. Cut out a piece of gingham fabric 2cm (¾in) wider than the window and 22cm (8¾in) deep.

I HOUR

You will need
- voile fabric
- scissors
- gingham fabric
- sewing machine or needle and cotton
- iron
- self-adhesive touch-and-close tape

2 Place the gingham strip and the voile with right sides together, matcing a long edge of the gingham with what will be the bottom edge of the voile. Sew together 1cm (⅜in) in from the edge. Iron out the seam. With the two fabrics joined, turn in 1cm (⅜in) hems on all edges, press and stitch.

3 Cut a strip of self-adhesive touch-and-close tape the width of the curtain panel. Fix one side of the touch-and-close tape to the top of the window frame and the other along the top back edge of the curtain. Press the two strips of touch-and-close tape together to fit the curtain in place.

Curtain tricks

Tea towel café curtains

Secure the length of net curtain wire across the window about halfway up, fixing it with screw hooks at either side. Hang the tea towels over the wire and hold them in place with wooden clothes pegs.

45 MINUTES

You will need
- net curtain wire
- screw hooks
- 2 tea towels
- wooden clothes pegs

Contrasting curtains

This is a simple way to make a longer curtain, ideal for curtains that have shrunk or have been moved to a taller window. Simply add a panel along the width of the bottom of each curtain in a contrasting fabric. Hem the panels and then stitch on to the bottom of the existing curtains.

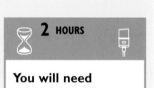

2 HOURS

You will need
- pair of curtains
- contrasting fabric
- tape measure
- scissors
- sewing machine or needle and cotton
- iron

Fleece tassel tie back

Cut the rectangle of fleece in half diagonally to make two triangles. Roll each triangle into a sausage shape, starting from the long edge and rolling towards the point, and secure with stitches. Sew a loop of thin cord to the top of each tassel. Roll two pieces of thin cord into discs and stitch one on to the front of each tassel. Hang on a length of thicker cord tied round the curtain.

 HOUR

You will need
- polyester fleece, 38x18cm (15x7in)
- scissors
- needle and cotton
- thin cord
- thick cord

Easy tie-up curtain

Measure and cut the fabric to fit the window, allowing an extra third on the width for gathering plus some more for hems. Use an iron to press hems around all sides, then fix in place with iron-on hem tape.

Using tailor's chalk or a pencil, mark the positions of the eyelets along the top edge of the curtain, about 15cm (6in) apart and about 2cm (¾in) in from the edge. Use the eyelet kit to fix the eyelets in place on the pencil marks. Thread short lengths of ribbon tape through the eyelets and fasten the curtain to the pole.

HOUR

You will need
- curtain fabric
- tape measure
- scissors
- iron
- iron-on hem tape
- tailor's chalk or pencil
- eyelet kit
- ribbon tape

Red and white

Pincer clip drapes

Measure and cut the fabric to fit the window, allowing an extra third on the width for gathering plus extra for hems. Use an iron to press hems around all sides, then fix in place with iron-on hem tape.

Turn the curtain face down on a flat surface. Use a ruler and tailor's chalk or a pencil to make marks on the curtain at 7.5cm (3in) intervals all along the top edge of the curtain. Next, fasten the pincer clips on to the marked points and attach the curtain rings to them.

⌛ 1 HOUR

You will need
- tape measure
- scissors
- curtain fabric
- iron
- iron-on hem tape
- ruler
- tailor's chalk or pencil
- pincer clips
- curtain rings

Shelf trim border

Dress up plain shelves with a fabric trim. Use a length of fabric, lace or ribbon, or a wallpaper border. Cut the border to the required length and simply stick in place using double-sided sticky tape or drawing pins.

⌛ 30 MINUTES

You will need
- fabric or wallpaper border
- tape measure
- scissors
- double-sided sticky tape or drawing pins

Fabric-covered books

Use coordinating fabrics in plain, checks and stripes to give books a decorative touch. Allow enough fabric to cover the entire book, adding an extra 5cm (2in) all round to stick down inside the book cover. Stick the fabric down with strong glue. Sew on buttons and tassel ties if desired.

 45 MINUTES

You will need
- fabric remnants
- books
- tape measure
- scissors
- strong glue
- buttons and tassel ties

Pretty window panel

Cut 20cm (8in) squares from the fabric and hem the edges using a needle and cotton or iron-on hem tape. Alternatively, use a number of pretty handkerchiefs or printed scarves.

Attach the squares to curtain clips and hang from a simple curtain pole or rod above the window.

 **2** HOURS

You will need
- floral print fabric, handkerchiefs or scarves
- tape measure
- scissors
- needle and cotton or iron-on hem tape
- curtain clips
- curtain pole

Fast cover-ups

Denim floor cushion

Cut out two circles of denim with a width of around 50cm (20in). Then cut a long strip of denim, about 20cm (8in) wide, long enough to fit the perimeter of the circles you have cut.

 2 HOURS

You will need
- denim fabric
- tape measure
- scissors
- pins
- sewing machine
- zip
- small pieces of foam or polystyrene balls to fill the cushion

With the right sides of the fabric together, pin the long length around each circle allowing a 2cm (¾in) seam and leaving space along one side to attach a zip. Pin the zip in place. Stitch around the pinned seams.

Turn the fabric cover the right side out and fill the cushion cover with small pieces of foam or polystyrene pieces until it is plump, and zip up.

Denim pillowcases

Measure an existing pillowcase and use it to give you the measurements for the fabric. Cut out two pieces of fabric, allowing an extra 2.5cm (1in) for hems, plus 15cm (6in) extra length on one piece for the pillow cuff.

 I HOUR

You will need
- tape measure
- denim or jersey fabric
- scissors
- pins
- sewing machine or needle and cotton
- buttons

Hem the cuff end of the longer piece of fabric, then lay it right side down on a flat surface. Fold over the 15cm (6in) cuff, pin the two sides and sew up. Next, hem one short side of the other piece of fabric. Place the two pieces together, right sides facing, and sew around three sides, leaving the cuffed and hemmed edges open. Turn right sides out and sew buttons along the cuffed front of the pillow.

Pattern hole blind

Draw your design on to tracing paper with a pencil, making sure it will fit on the blind. Stick to simple shapes which will be easy to cut out.

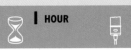

You will need
- tracing paper
- soft pencil
- plain roller blind
- cutting mat
- craft knife

Place the tracing paper pencil-side down on the wrong side of the blind. Scribble over the outline of the design so that it transfers the pencil marks on to the blind. Place a cutting mat under the blind and cut out the design with a craft knife. Fix the blind in place on the window.

Revamped dining chairs

Remove the seat pads and lightly sand the chairs to remove any varnish and provide a key for the paint. Wipe over with white spirit to remove any dirt and grease. Paint the chair with a coat of primer and leave to dry. Then apply several coats of emulsion. When the paint is dry, rub beeswax into the chair frame and buff to a shine with a soft cloth.

HOUR per chair plus drying

You will need
- chairs
- sandpaper
- white spirit and cloth
- paintbrush
- wood primer
- emulsion paint
- beeswax
- soft cloth
- fabric
- scissors
- staple gun

Cut enough fabric to cover the seat pad, allowing 10cm (4in) extra all round to tuck under. Cover the seat pad with the fabric and turn it face down. Fold the fabric over the front edge of the seat and fix in place with a staple gun on the bottom of the seat. Pull the fabric taut and fold it over the back edge of the seat, and fix with the staple gun. Fold the corners in place and staple, then work your way around the seat with the staple gun, keeping the fabric taut as you go. Replace the seat pad.

American country

Mix red, white and blue to create a striking scheme reminiscent of the American dream. Keep patterns simple – stripes and checks were popular – and be inspired by traditional crafts such as quilting and patchwork.

▼   Update plain cushions by sewing large panels of patterned fabric to the front.

▲   Use a collection of fabric remnants to make up a really individual quilt for a bed or sofa.

▲   Make a cosy, oversize throw from broad bands of plain-coloured blanket or fleece sewn together.

▲　Arm slips for your sofa are practical and create fresh interest. Make your own by hemming pretty, loose rectangles of fabric.

▲　Combine simple patterns such as large and small checks in different colours and stripes in different directions for a cosy feel.

▲　Keep drawers smelling fresh. Sew together pouches of fabrics and fill with lavender. Checks, stripes and ginghams enhance the country look.

Blue and white

Always fresh and attractive, blue and white is a fail-safe classic combination. Most blues mix well together and with the added crispness of white look good in a multitude of styles.

▼ Make a simple laundry bag with a drawstring to hook on the back of a door.

▲ Make a cushion cover with two pieces of denim and add decorative wooden buttons for a finishing touch.

▲ Checked and striped fabrics in blues and whites work wonderfully together in a plain white room, to add colour and pattern.

▲ Textured and patterned wallpapers are a good way of adding colour if plain blue walls alone feel too bold for you. They play a similar role to fabrics in a room scheme.

▲ A collection of fabrics in similar shades of blue will always work together.

▲ Combine stripes, plains, checks and patterns to give the room depth and interest.

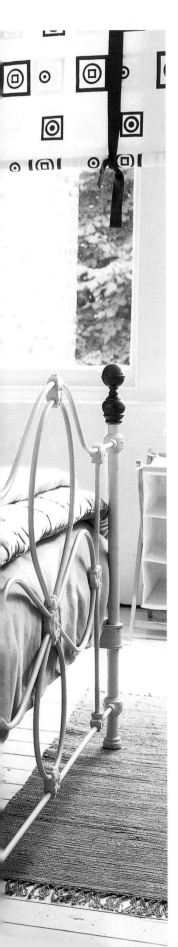

Lavender blue guestroom

Mix crisp white linen with shades of lavender blue and touches of silver for a striking guest bedroom.

The bed, with its iron bedstead and many-textured layers is the main feature of the room. Opt for fairly plain bedlinen – this features a pretty border detail – and add piles of cushions, quilts and throws. Different textures like satin, cotton and mohair all help to give the bed a soft and sumptuous finish.

The walls above the white-painted wood panelling are a calming lavender blue, with a pretty silver border added just above the rail. A blind with blue ribbon at the window gives privacy and is a simple finishing touch.

Natural floorboards add a slightly rustic touch, finished with a seagrass rug. Storage crates and under-bed baskets create extra storage space if needed. Finally, add pretty finishing touches such as a bedside lamp, scented candles and pretty toiletries.

What else would work?

- cream or oatmeal carpet
- white floorboards
- silver or chrome iron bed
- simple border of a straight line or geometric pattern

▲ Give plain walls a touch of pattern with a simple border in silver.

▲ Simple Shaker-style peg rails offer extra hanging space while a floorstanding rail houses towels.

▲ An old table can be transformed with a lick of silver paint.

Mediterranean living room

Capture the vibrant, fresh feel of the Mediterranean with a crisp blue, brilliant white and zesty yellow scheme.

You can't beat brilliant Mediterranean colours for a clear and vibrant look – mix azure and cobalt blues with stark white and yellow for fresh contrast. To give the room a Mediterranean feel, simple, patterned cushions have been added to the comfortable, yellow sofa. A soft and cosy throw gives the sofa a snug effect. Bright blue walls provide a wonderful contrast, while the glowing yellow of the long, plain curtains and boldly patterned cushions on the sofa highlight the sun-drenched Mediterranean look.

A voile curtain is hung café style at the window, allowing light to flood in. White floorboards enhance the fresh feel which can be finished with a stripy blue rug for softness underfoot. Rattan and white wood furniture are perfect for this look. Finally, add accessories in blues, whites and yellows – coloured glass and mosaic would also look wonderful.

What else would work?

- yellow walls with a blue sofa
- soft yellow carpet
- delicate floral curtains in blue, white and yellow

▲ Choose colourful decorative accessories to work with this look. Mosaic and brightly coloured flowers add the perfect decoration.

▲ Rattan furniture, even in the form of a simple armchair, adds a charming rustic touch.

▲ Choose brightly coloured cushions to bring a plain sofa alive. Here various shades of blue work wonders.

▲ Use a combination of fabric patterns for a casual effect but avoid too many large prints or the room will start looking fussy.

▲ Clear mid-blues work well in a contemporary environment but they look great in a more traditional setting too.

▲ Fabrics in traditional checks and ginghams are perfect for accentuating the country style look.

Country chic

A naturally inspired combination of blues and creams creates a fresh welcoming feel.

This cosy country theme relies on fresh blues and warm creams. The key ingredient here, apart from the colour element, is mixing patterns together. A scattering of checks and stripes in different sizes gives the room a fresh modern twist, sticking to blue and white shades. Texture can also be used to make the room inviting. A traditional three-piece suite in cream can be combined with an armchair in blue and white check for contrast. Distressed furniture is also perfect for this country look. A plain carpet works best in this scheme. Choose a cream or oatmeal tone; a slightly textured effect is perfect. Add accessories such as vases and cushions to help give the room extra texture and to stop it looking too plain. Choose accessories in blue, cream and splashes of chocolate brown. Break up a large area of wall using paint and wallpaper, or even a combination of both, above and below a dado rail. A dado rail works very well with this look. Choose a creamy shade above the dado and a fresh mid-toned blue shade below.

What else would work?

- distressed furniture
- carpets with small, simple patterns
- old polished wood floor with rugs
- simple cream walls

New naturals

Neutral and natural schemes create a calm environment that's versatile and simple to achieve. There's a whole choice of colours to be used, from creams through taupe, beige and fawn to richer coffee shades. White gives a bright, fresh feel, creamier tones add softness and warmth while coffee and chocolate tones mixed with soft creams can create a sophisticated look. For a more dramatic effect, add splashes of deep brown and black; even mid-blues can work as an accent in a natural scheme. Neutrals look at home in both traditional and contemporary settings. Opt for natural fabrics such as calico, muslin, hessian and coir to perfect the natural look and provide contrasting textures too.

Stylish banners

Create a stylish window treatment with simple fabric banners. The finished effect is modern and striking.

1 Fix the short brackets to the wall adjacent to the window frame on either side and about 5cm (2in) from the top. Fix the longer brackets level with the top of the window frame and about 5cm (2in) out from the shorter brackets. Saw the chrome poles to size.

2 Cut two pieces of calico, each roughly one third of the width of the longer pole, plus an extra 4cm (1½in) for hems. These should be long enough to reach the floor from the lower pole; allow 18cm (7in) for hems.

3 Fold over 2cm (¾in) hems at the sides of the banners, sew and press. Turn over and press a 1cm (⅜in) hem at top and bottom, then fold over and stitch a 6cm (2½in) hem at the top of each panel, leaving the ends open to create a channel for the pole. Make a 10cm (4in) hem at the bottom of each banner and sew in place.

4 Measure two banners from the patterned fabric, each roughly one quarter of the width of the longer pole and long enough to reach the floor from the upper pole. Allow for hems as with the calico.

5 Fold under 0.5cm (⅛in), then 1.5cm (⅝in) along each long edge and stitch in place. Fold under 1cm (⅜in),

6 HOURS

You will need
• a pair of short curtain rail brackets
• drill
• screws
• screwdriver
• a pair of long curtain rail brackets
• 2 chrome poles, 2.5cm (1in) thick
• hacksaw
• calico fabric
• tape measure
• scissors
• sewing machine or needle and cotton
• iron
• patterned fabric

then 6cm (2½in) at the top edge and stitch in place, making a channel as before. Fold under 1cm (⅜in), then 10cm (4in) at the bottom of the banner, then stitch in place. Press all the hems.

6 Hang the calico banners on the shorter, lower rail and the patterned fabric banners on the longer rail. Fit the chrome poles into the brackets.

Bedroom wall hanging

Make a pretty backdrop for your bed with a length of fabric to coordinate with the bedlinen. It's a cheap and instant way of making an effective focal point for your bed.

1 Cut the fabric to make a rectangle that is roughly three-quarters of the width of your bed and reaches from the ceiling to the bottom of the bedhead. Turn over and hem all four edges. Press well.

2 Attach the curtain pole to the top of the wall behind the bed, making sure it is fixed centrally above the bed.

3 Attach curtain clips to the fabric panel and hang on the curtain rail letting the fabric drop behind the bed or bedhead.

4 To give added substance to the hanging you could line it or even quilt it (for which you will need a length of wadding the same size as the hanging). Alternatively, you could add a contrasting border or sew wool fringing across the top and down the sides.

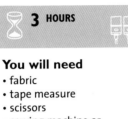

3 HOURS

You will need
- fabric
- tape measure
- scissors
- sewing machine or needle and cotton
- iron
- curtain pole and brackets
- drill
- screws
- screwdriver
- curtain clips

Rustic table cover

Conceal a messy area under a coffee table with a rustic fabric slipcover. Add pockets and you'll have a hiding place for the daily paper and the TV remote control.

1 Measure the height, depth and width of the table. When transferring the measurements on to the fabric, check that the pattern will match up at all the seams when the cover is sewn up. Cut out five pieces of fabric, one for each side and one for the top of the table, adding an extra 1.5cm (⅝in) on all sides for seams. Cut out two pieces of fabric for the pockets – they can be any size you want, but making them large enough to hold a magazine is useful.

⏳ **2–3 HOURS**

You will need
- tape measure
- fabric
- scissors
- sewing machine or needle and cotton
- iron

2 Turn under and sew a narrow hem around three sides of the pocket rectangles. On the fourth side, which will be the top, turn under 0.5cm (³⁄₁₆in) and then 1.5cm (⅝in). Sew in place and press.

3 With right sides together, stitch two opposite side pieces to the top piece – if the table is oblong, these should be the shorter sides. Add a pocket to both ends. Join the two other side pieces to the top to form a cross shape, then stitch all four side seams together. Press all the seams flat and hem the bottom. Iron the cover and slip it over the table.

Textural hessian curtain

Hessian makes an inexpensive curtain treatment and adds a lovely textured feel to a neutral room scheme.

1 Cut a rectangle of fabric to fit the window, allowing an extra 2cm (¾in) all round for hems. Next, cut four strips for the border, two for the long sides of the curtain and two for the short sides. The strips need to be double the width of the border required, plus an extra 4cm (1½in) for hems. On the length, allow extra for the length and width the border will add. A 10cm (4in) border, for example, will increase the overall dimensions of the curtain by 20cm (8in) each way.

3 HOURS

You will need
- tape measure
- hessian fabric
- scissors
- pins
- sewing machine or needle and cotton
- eyelet kit
- length of rope
- 2 curtain holdbacks
- drill
- screws
- screwdriver

2 Fold one of the border strips in half lengthways and place over the edge of the curtain panel to work out the positioning. Fold under 1cm (⅜in) hem and pin, then sew the border, right sides facing, to the front of the curtain. Fold the corners into a mitre, then fold the strip over to the wrong side of the curtain and sew in place. Repeat with the other strips, then carefully handstitch the mitred corners.

3 Fix a row of equally spaced eyelets along the top border of the curtain. Then thread the length of rope through the eyelets.

4 Fix the curtain holdbacks to the wall, one on each side of the window at the top. Tie the rope around the two holdbacks to secure the curtain in place.

Buttons and beads

Beaded tie-back

Measure the distance around the bunched-up curtain to work out how long the tie-back needs to be. Cut a leather thong or length of wire to size, then thread on a selection of beads in contrasting natural colours and different shapes. Secure the beads on to the leather or wire by tying the ends in a knot.

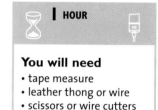

⏳ **1 HOUR**

You will need
- tape measure
- leather thong or wire
- scissors or wire cutters
- beads
- screw-in hook (optional)

Wrap the tie-back around the curtain and tie in a knot or bow. Alternatively, form a loop at each end and fix to a hook screwed into the window frame.

Tab-top curtains

Measure two lengths of muslin to fit the window. Hem the curtains on all sides. To make the tabs, cut strips of fabric that are twice as wide and twice as long as you want the tabs to be. Fold the strips in half lengthways, fold in the raw edges and stitch the tabs to the curtain. Press the tabs.

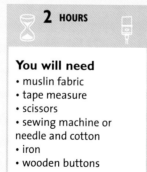

⏳ **2 HOURS**

You will need
- muslin fabric
- tape measure
- scissors
- sewing machine or needle and cotton
- iron
- wooden buttons

Finally, sew a wooden button to the curtain at the bottom of each tab.

Button design curtain

Cut out paper circles as templates to plan the design on your curtains. Lay each curtain panel flat and position the paper circles randomly over the curtain.

2 HOURS

You will need
• scrap paper
• scissors
• plain curtains
• pencil or tailor's chalk
• needle and cotton
• wooden and mother of pearl buttons

Once you are happy with the effect, draw round the edges of the circles with a pencil or tailor's chalk.

Using a double thread in your needle, stitch some buttons on to the curtains within one of the marked circles. Repeat to fill each circle.

Button cushion cover

Remove the cushion from the cushion cover. Work out a button design along the centre of the cushion, working from one side to the other. Mark in pencil or tailor's chalk where each button should go. Sew the

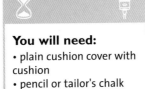

1 HOUR

You will need:
• plain cushion cover with cushion
• pencil or tailor's chalk
• wooden buttons
• needle and cotton

wooden buttons on to the cover, following the design. The buttons can be sewn in straight lines or placed more randomly.

Nature's treasures

Appliqué apple frame

Cut a 3mm (⅛in) thick slice of apple and sandwich it between two pieces of kitchen paper, then two pieces of plywood. Put it in a microwave and place a non-metallic weight on top. Heat for 3 minutes on a medium setting. Take out and leave to cool. Continue to heat the apple for periods of 20 seconds, leaving it to cool and changing the paper from time to time to absorb the moisture. Watch out for signs of burning.

When the apple slice is almost dried out, put it on a piece of kitchen paper on a warm radiator or sunny windowsill to dry out completely.

Cut a square of muslin fabric and sew on to the card using a sewing machine and coloured cotton. Mount the apple slice on top and place in the frame.

⏳	I HOUR plus drying	🖌

You will need
- apple
- knife
- kitchen paper
- 2 small sheets of plywood
- microwave
- muslin fabric
- scissors
- sewing machine and coloured cotton
- picture frame
- handmade card to fit frame
- glue

Leaf design print

Cut the fabric into a rectangle slightly smaller than the picture frame. Cut a piece of thin card to fit the frame, press the fabric and mount it on to the card with glue.

Cut a piece of mount board to fit the frame, then use a ruler and pencil to mark out the window on the back of the board. The window should be placed centrally. Lay the mount board on the cutting mat and use the craft knife and a metal ruler to cut out the window. Set the mount over the fabric and fit in to the frame.

⏳	30 MINUTES	🖌

You will need
- fabric with leaf design
- scissors
- thin card
- iron
- strong glue
- mount board
- metal ruler
- pencil
- cutting mat
- craft knife
- picture frame

Hessian-covered vase

Measure the height and circumference of the vase and cut a piece of hessian to fit, allowing an extra 2.5cm (1in) at the bottom and 4cm (1½in) at the top. Fray the top 4cm (1½in) of the hessian by removing the horizontal threads.

20 MINUTES

You will need
- plain vase
- tape measure
- hessian
- scissors
- strong glue

Carefully stick the hessian around the vase with strong glue, tucking 2.5cm (1in) underneath the vase. Fill the vase with dried stems in natural colours for a pretty arrangement.

Feather frames

First measure the clip frames and cut out a piece of handmade paper to fit each, using a craft knife and cutting mat.

Use glue to stick a feather in the centre of each piece of handmade paper and allow to dry. Once dry, mount the pieces of paper in the clip frames and hang the frames in a row, equally spaced.

20 minutes

You will need
- ruler
- three clip frames
- handmade paper
- pencil
- craft knife
- cutting mat
- large feathers
- glue

Natural appeal

When working within the limited palette of natural hues, the importance of texture becomes obvious. Look for interesting weaves and finishes, and play up the subtle differences in texture that become more apparent without the interplay of contrasting colours.

▲ Create a pretty picture for the wall by cutting out a piece of appliquéd fabric to fit a wooden picture frame. Add a plain border to finish the edges and fix into the frame.

▼ Coarse weaves, such as hessian, are even more characterful with the light behind them.

▲ Update a plain and simple paper lampshade by gluing on artificial flowers. Cut the heads from their stems, and then fix to the shade using strong glue.

▲ Add pattern and texture with subtle coloured wallpapers and borders. Hung in panels or rows, these help to add interest to a neutral scheme.

▲ Textured floor coverings work wonderfully in natural room schemes. They add texture and are available in a whole range of neutral colours.

▲ There is nothing like real linen to set off a dining table. Make a pocket for knives and forks by folding the napkin and turning under the sides.

Chocolate and cream

A combination of soft creams, caramels and deep chocolate creates a dramatic scheme. Give pale neutrals an edge with rich, dark chocolate, and offset deep browns with clear, light tones of clotted cream, straw and parchment.

▼   For a decorative tie-back, cut a piece of rope long enough to hold the curtain and add a linen tassel to finish.

▲   Give plain throws a luxurious look by sewing a velvet border around the edges. Extend the border to the back so the throw is reversible.

▲   Add tonal colour to a plain scheme by covering the seats of sofas and armchairs in a coordinating fabric.

▲ For a sophisticated curtain holdback, fix a decorative glass doorknob to the wall to hold the curtains in place.

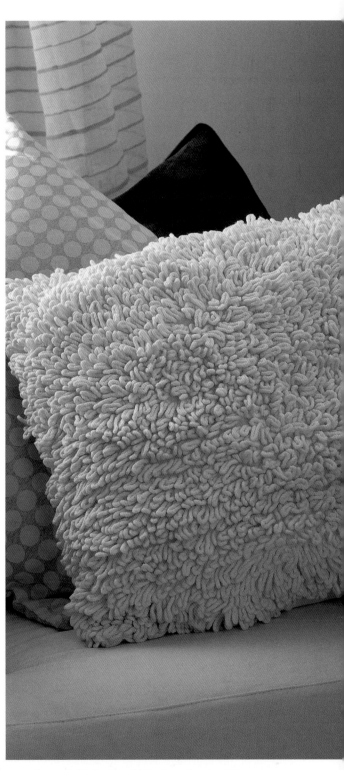

▲ Make your own cushion covers in a variety of different toning shades. Use textured fabrics to add depth to plain rooms.

▲ For a fluffy textured effect, make a cushion cover from an old bath mat using a heavy-duty cotton to sew it together.

Rich coffee lounge

A combination of rich brown and soft cream with natural wood creates a modern, easy-to-live-with atmosphere a world away from a hotel lounge.

The room's focus, the sofa, is brought to life with a large modern print throw, which adds a touch of simple pattern to this plain neutral room. A woven pattern would also work well here. Velvet cushions in deep coffee shades add a feeling of cosiness and luxury.

The walls are painted in a soft cream to enhance the neutral, calm background feel. A wood floor works ideally with this look – choose mid to rich, dark toned woods for contrast with the cream. Simple, sculptural ceramics look great in this scheme. Build up a mixed collection in all tones, from latté to espresso. A bamboo coffee table with a dark wood finish extends the range of textures, while dried grasses or flowers underline the natural theme.

What else would work?

- natural floor-covering such as sisal
- textured carpet in an oatmeal shade
- walls in two different shades, such as buttermilk and fawn
- calico or hessian blind

▲ Velvet cushions add a rich, luxurious feel to this simple and inexpensive look.

▲ Wooden accessories, such as picture frames, add to the natural feel.

▲ This throw has been made by dyeing a plain sheet dark brown, then using white fabric paint and a stamp to create the white squares.

Checks and balances

Mix soft beige, fawn and cream for a cosy bedroom with plenty of pattern and texture.

A variety of checks are combined to great effect here. The repeated tones of café au lait and cream allow the checkered bedinen to mix happily with the smaller check of the valance and matching tab-top curtains (not shown). The theme is echoed in the subtle patterning in the bedside rug and the large decorative patches on the spare blanket.

Contrasts in textures make a big contribution to the success of this scheme: smooth cotton bedlinen against the chunky knitted throw, the soft rug on the pleasing rustic roughness of the sisal carpet.

Keep furniture and accessories simple. A rattan basket or blanket box at the end of the bed provides a practical storage solution, while adding extra texture. Store blankets and cushions inside as well as on top for added decoration. A simple canvas wardrobe like this fits in well with the style of the room. Look for finishing touches that are well made but unfussy, in tones from cream and fawn to toffee and bitter chocolate.

What else would work?

- cream or oatmeal textured carpet
- simple stripes on bedlinen and cushions
- rattan furniture

▲ A chocolate-coloured lampshade provides subtle contrast to the scheme.

▲ A patterned throw with patchwork squares creates a cosy country feel while adding a touch of bolder pattern.

▲ A canvas wardrobe makes an alternative to wooden or rattan furniture. It is inexpensive, so ideal if you are trying to keep your budget down.

Fresh florals

Pretty-patterned florals create a classic and evocative effect. They are often considered to be old fashioned, but this needn't be so. There are a multitude of floral-inspired patterns available, from traditional chintzes to striking modern designs. There is no rule that says florals should only be used with traditional colours – introduce a bold colour to give a new and exciting twist.

Floral fabrics can create different looks, from soft and romantic, to fresh summery schemes. Florals alone can be overpowering, so team them with coordinating checks, stripes or plains.

Pretty pocket curtain

Decorate the curtains in a child's bedroom with pretty fabric remnants to make handy storage pockets for small toys.

1 To make the fabric pockets, cut a selection of rectangles from floral fabric remnants. Cut as many pockets as you need to cover the curtains and vary the sizes to add visual interest.

6 HOURS

You will need
- floral fabric remnants
- scissors
- iron
- sewing machine and cotton
- plain curtains
- pins

2 Make a 1cm (⅜in) cut in from each corner of each fabric rectangle. Next, fold a 1cm (⅜in) hem on both the long edges and one of the short edges of each piece and press. On the remaining short side, press a 1cm (⅜in) hem, then fold over again and iron to form the pocket top. Machine stitch across each pocket top, to hold the hem.

3 Lay each curtain panel, right side up, on a flat surface. Arrange the pockets, right side up, on top of the fabric panel and position them randomly. Once you are happy with the effect, pin the pockets in place, then machine stitch, sewing down one long side, across the base of each pocket, then up the remaining long side, taking care to stitch close to the outside edge.

Rose bedlinen

Add panels of bold, rose-covered fabric to plain bedlinen
to create a cosy country look.

1 Cut a square to the desired size from the floral fabric. Use an iron to press 1cm (⅜in) hems on the wrong side of all four edges.

2 Pin the square, right side up, to the centre of the duvet cover. Secure the edges by slipping a length of iron-on hem tape under each edge and pressing in place.

3 Next, measure a pillowcase and cut a rectangle of the floral fabric 10cm (4in) smaller all round. Tuck under the edges and attach the fabric to the pillowcase with iron-on hem tape, as before.

 **4 HOURS**

You will need
- rose-pattern fabric
- scissors
- tape measure
- plain duvet cover and pillowcases
- iron
- pins
- iron-on hem tape

Voile bed canopy

Give your bedroom a colonial feel with a summery swag, adding a touch of elegance to your room and make a feature of the bed.

1 First screw the two pairs of hooks into the ceiling from which to hang the dowel supports. Position the first two above the head of the bed, setting them apart about 2cm (¾in) wider than the fabric. Screw in the hooks over the bottom of the bed in line with the two at the top of the bed. Tie a length of cord on each of the hooks and suspend two of the lengths of dowelling by the cords, one at either end of the bed, using a spirit level to check they are horizontal.

2 Cut a length of fabric to reach from the floor behind the top of the bed, up over the two dowels and half way to the floor again at the foot of the bed. Press and sew a double hem at one end of the fabric. At the other end, turn under and press a 1cm (⅜in) hem, then turn under another 3cm (1¼in) and stitch to form a channel. Cut the third dowelling to length and slip through the channel in the fabric to act as a weight.

3 Hang the fabric over the two dowelling supports so the weighted end hangs behind the top of the bed. Tie the free end of the fabric in a loose knot, or alternatively let the free end hang loosely over the other end.

2 HOURS

You will need
- 4 screw-in hooks
- tape measure
- about 4m (4⅓ yards) of cord
- scissors
- 3 pieces of dowelling, 12mm (½in) thick
- saw
- spirit level
- about 4.5m (5 yards) of voile fabric
- iron
- sewing machine and cotton

Tie-top bed drapes

Give a four-poster bed a pretty finish with tie-top drapes.

1 Measure the height and width of the bed to work out the size of the main curtain. It will probably be necessary to join two widths of fabric together. The side curtains are just for show, so a single width of fabric for each side should be fine.

⏳ **6 HOURS**

You will need
- tape measure
- fabric for fronts of curtains
- fabric for backs of curtains
- scissors
- fabric for ties
- iron
- sewing machine or needle and cotton
- pins

2 Cut a back and a front for each of the three curtains, allowing extra for seams. Check the backs and fronts of the curtains match in size.

3 Cut strips of contrasting fabric to make the ties. They should be roughly 5x55cm (2x22in). Press each strip in half lengthways, open out and fold in the raw edges. Press again to form narrow strips about 1.5cm (⅝in) wide. Stitch to close the folded edges. At one end of each tie, tuck the raw edges in and stitch across the end.

4 Lay the back of each curtain right side up on a work surface and pin pairs of ties along the top edge. Space the ties at 15cm (6in) intervals with the raw edges aligned with the top of the curtain and the ties themselves laying on the fabric.

5 Lay the fronts of the curtains on top, right side down with the sides aligned. Sew around all edges to join the fronts and backs together, leaving a gap in one of the seams. Turn the curtains right sides out through the gap, then handstitch the gap closed and press the curtains.

Floral pelmet

Specially designed PVC for pelmets offers an easy way to add a traditional feel to your windows.

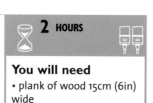

1 Cut the wood so it is 10cm (4in) longer than the width of the window frame. Screw one bracket on to each end of the piece of wood, with their inner edges 5cm (2in) from the ends so they will butt up against the outer edges of the window frame. Screw the brackets to the wall, one on either side of the window frame and place the piece of wood on the brackets like a shelf and screw in position.

⏳ **2 HOURS**

You will need
• plank of wood 15cm (6in) wide
• tape measure
• saw
• 2 shelf brackets
• screws
• screwdriver
• drill
• fabric
• scissors
• double-sided adhesive PVC
• self-adhesive touch-and-close tape

2 Cut a length of adhesive PVC to form the pelmet front and sides. Smooth the wrong side of the fabric on to one side of the adhesive PVC. Turn the PVC over, remove the backing paper and fold the excess edges of the fabric on to the sticky base. Cut a piece of fabric to cover the back of the PVC.

3 Stick one side of the self-adhesive touch-and-close tape along the front and side edges of the wood. Remove the fuzzy strip and stick this to the back of the pelmet along the top edge. Attach the pelmet to the wood.

Decorative screen

A decorative screen is a great way to conceal a messy place or create a changing area. It also adds a decorative element to a bedroom.

1 Remove the hinges from the screen to make three separate panels. Cut a piece of fabric large enough to cover each side of each of the three panels with a good bit to spare. Lay one piece of fabric on the floor, right side down, and lay one of the screen panels on top, making sure the pattern on the fabric is aligned properly with the screen. Cut the fabric around the panel, about 7.5cm (3in) from the edges.

6 HOURS

You will need
- solid folding MDF screen
- screwdriver
- fabric
- scissors
- staple gun
- decorative hook or knob

2 Stretch the edges of the fabric over on to the top of the panel and staple in place, making the edges as neat as possible on the curves.

3 Lay another piece of fabric right sides up on the panel and cut to fit the panel with an extra 1cm (⅜in) on all sides. Turn under the raw edges and staple the fabric to the panel. This will be the back.

4 Repeat with the other two panels, then replace the hinges to hold the screen together. Fix a hook or knob to the front of the screen to hang clothes or bags, for a decorative look.

Seat treatments

Flowery cushions

Recycle pillows by making fabric covers for them and turning them into handsome rectangular cushions, which look effective placed lengthways on a sofa. First measure the pillow and cut two pieces of fabric the same size, adding an extra 10cm (4in) to the length and 4cm (1½in) to the width.

45 MINUTES

You will need
• pillow
• tape measure
• floral fabric
• scissors
• sewing machine or needle and cotton
• iron
• press studs

Lay the two pieces of fabric one on top of the other with right sides facing. Sew a 2cm (¾in) hem round the two long sides and one short side. Turn back a 2cm (¾in) hem at the open end and sew in place. Stitch on three or four press studs. Turn the cover right sides out and insert the pillow.

Scented pocket cushion

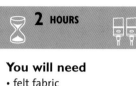

2 HOURS

Cut two pieces of felt to fit the cushion. Lay the two pieces side by side and sew in the zip to join them. Topstitch with a decorative stitch in a contrasting coloured cotton. Cut a small square of felt to make the pocket and sew on one side of the cushion cover with decorative stitch, leaving the top open.

You will need
• felt fabric
• scissors
• sewing machine and cotton
• pins
• zip
• floral fabric
• lavender

Sew around the other three sides, again using the decorative stitch for contrast.

Make a small floral pouch to fit inside the pocket, making it slightly longer than the pocket so it sticks out a bit at the top. Sew three edges of the pouch and fill with lavender. Handstitch the fourth edge to close, then place inside the felt pocket.

Floral chair cover

Measure the seat of the chair, then cut out a piece of fabric big enough to cover it, allowing an extra 20cm (8in) all around.

Place the fabric, face down, over the chair and mark where the top corners of the chair seat come.

45 MINUTES

You will need
• tape measure
• floral fabric
• scissors
• pencil or tailor's chalk
• sewing machine or needle and cotton
• iron

Remove the fabric and cut a diagonal line from each corner to the nearest mark. Now hem all sides of the fabric and along the diagonal cuts. Place the cover over the chair seat.

Embroidered borders

Measure the cushion and cut the embroidered trim to fit along all four edges. Pin and sew into place.

Measure the throw and cut the wide ribbon to fit all four sides. Fold in half lengthways and pin into place to cover the edges of the throw, with half on the front and half on the back of the throw. Stitch to secure.

Now pin some lengths of embroidered trim along the inside edge of the ribbon on the front of the throw and stitch into place.

2 HOURS

You will need
• cushion and cover
• tape measure
• embroidered lace trim
• scissors
• pins
• needle and cotton
• matching throw
• velvet or silk ribbon

Romantic touches

Great overblown peonies and roses, sweet sprigs of rose buds, scatterings of wild meadow flowers: mix and match them with abandon to create a soft, romantic look – and don't forget to bring real flowers into the room too.

▼ Mix plain pinks and creams with florals for a romantic effect.

▲ Make a quick and pretty decoration with glass jars, decorative ribbon and flowers. Simply tie ribbon around the necks of the jars and fill with fresh flowers.

▲ Give your bed a romantic country look by mixing layers of coordinating floral fabrics, in large and small prints, so they combine seamlessly together.

▲ Create a neat arm slipcover in a plain fabric to coordinate with the sofa and armchair. If your sofa is plain, use a floral fabric. Simply hem a rectangular panel and sew on pockets at one end to hold newspapers and small items.

▲ Make a simple seat cover from leftover curtain or cushion fabric to blend in with the room scheme.

▲ Enliven a floral cushion by adding plain borders in a strong colour.

A hint of blue

Choose blue-based fabrics for a twist on traditional florals. Most florals are associated with chintzy, rose-style prints; however, using blue floral patterns can add an interesting look, especially when teamed with checks or stripes.

▼ Create storage boxes that tie in with the rest of your room by covering them with leftover fabric or wallpaper.

▲ Update traditional floral curtains with a modern denim blind. Choose a special blind fabric or apply a stiffener to thin fabric, and use a simple rollerblind kit.

▲ Keep shoes tidy when they aren't being worn by making simple bags from pretty material. Sew on a length of ribbon to coordinate with the fabric.

▲ Bring an old chair to life by covering it with floral fabric cushions in a variety of patterns and styles.

▲ Give floral curtains an unusual finish by using leather curtain clips. Once you have hemmed the curtains, fix the leather clips to the tops and hang from a pole.

▲ Choose multicoloured floral prints for a funkier scheme. This reversible bedlinen has a coordinating striped design on the other side.

Dainty and delicate

Flower designs come as light, airy sprigs as well as luscious multi-petalled bouquets. Intricate floral patterns are ideal for smaller rooms as they are less likely to overwhelm. For a subtle effect, choose accessories to introduce these pretty patterns.

▼   Cover wooden coat hangers with wadding and fabric remnants to coordinate with the room.

▲   Give an old table a fresh look with a simple slipcover made from a remnant of fabric.

▲   Make your own scented pillows with leftover fabric from curtains or cushions. Fill with pot pourri and tie with coordinating velvet or satin ribbon.

▲ Mix and match fabrics and choose paints in soft to deep pinks, depending on how bold a look you want to create.

▲ Give plain white bedlinen a decorative touch by sewing on appliqué rose buds or flowers.

▲ Cover storage boxes with wallpaper or floral wrapping paper to match the curtains.

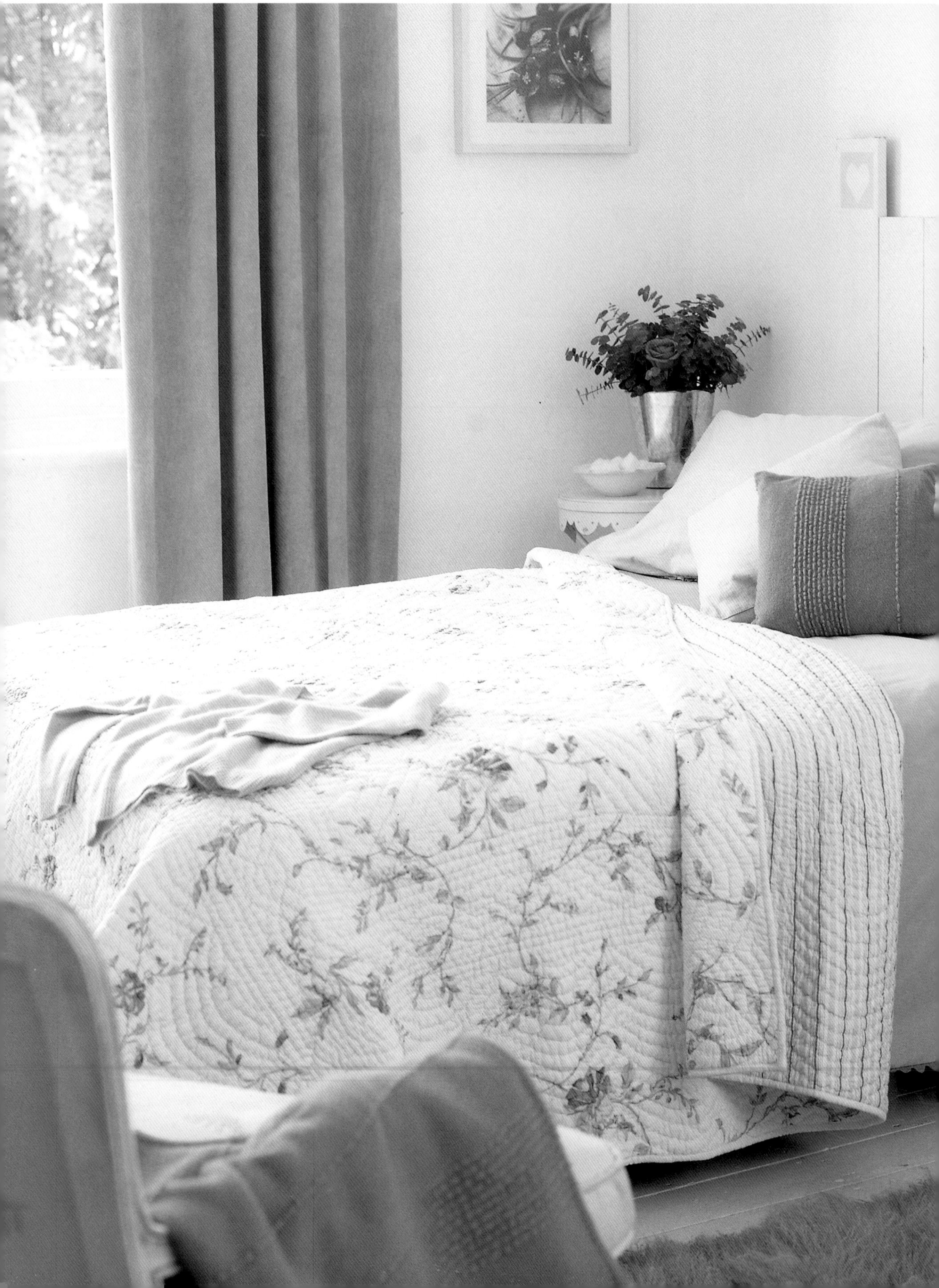

Soft lilac bedroom

Create a romantic bedroom with a colour palette of gentle, muted tones and delicate floral fabrics.

To achieve this delicate, layered look, begin by opting for pale lilac or pink bedlinen in a plain design. Soft details, such as a delicate lace trimming are perfectly suited to this look. An old-fashioned floral quilt really helps to define this style and the quilting adds texture to the bed. Choose a quilt in colours that work with the pink and lilac colour scheme – a touch of deeper, dusky pink is ideal for subtle accent colour. Add piles of decorative cushions in different textures to the top of the bed, choosing deeper dusky pinks, lilacs and pale pinks. A touch of baby blue can be added here too.

Paint the walls a warm lilac of a similar pale tone; steer away from anything too bright. Pale floorboards and wood or white-painted furniture is best suited to this look. Add a deep pile rug to accentuate the sumptuous feel and finish with pretty flowers and pictures.

What else would work?

- old pieces of furniture painted white
- thick velvety carpet in soft blue or pale pink
- delicate, modern prints on the walls

▲ Piles of cushions are an inexpensive way of adding a touch of luxury and cosiness to a room. Choose different shades and mix plains and patterns together.

▲ Fresh flowers add romance and softness to the room. Look out for silk and dried variations.

▲ Velvet curtains add to the luxuriant, romantic feel. For an opulent effect, choose velvet curtains in a deeper, dusky pink colour.

Modern floral

Combine traditional floral prints with shocking pinks for a new twist on a cosy country look.

This room mixes traditional touches with contemporary colour; country chintz is set against shocking pink for bold impact. Deep pink voile curtains add contrast and sofas have been covered in deep pink velvet textured fabric to contrast with an armchair in a traditional floral chintz. The soft cream carpet echoes the antique cream background on the walls.

The walls have been covered with tongue-and-groove panelling up to the dado rail for a really cosy cottage feel. To enhance the rustic effect, give them a distressed finish. Paint the walls above the dado in a soft, antique cream emulsion. As an alternative to wallpaper, two decorative flowerbud stamps have been used to decorate the walls, using pale green and pink paint for the flower and stem. Cherry wood furniture adds warm tones and a traditional feel. Add rustic accessories such as rattan baskets for storage. Frame pictures in cherry wood frames to match the furniture and add plenty of cushions for comfort. Accessories in dusky pink and green complete the look.

What else would work?

- plain walls, without tongue and groove
- pale green carpet
- plain sofas with chintz cushions

▲ An armchair covered in a traditional chintz fabric adds a cosy old-fashioned feel to this room, and the colours work perfectly with the main colour scheme.

▲ A sofa covered in velvet damask adds texture and colour to the room.

▲ Fabric swatches make a pretty subject for picture frames. Cut out a small square from a fabric that features in the room and frame it.

Pretty pastels

Pastel shades create a wonderfully calm and fresh scheme which is easy on the eye. There is a wide colour palette to choose from and you'll find plenty of soft furnishings to work with this style. From delicate prints, stripes and mixed checks to plain and textured fabrics, the choice is endless and you really can have fun mixing different patterns and colour combinations. Pastels work in layers and are ideal for creating a calming environment. Blues, pinks, aquas and lilacs go well together, and delicate yellow and soft apple greens provide a refreshing, summery feel. Because pastels are relaxing and undemanding, they are fun to work with and easy to live with.

Appliqué bedlinen

Give plain sheets and pillowcases a new look with bright appliqué circles and embroidery threads.

1 Use a pencil and a circular object to draw circles on to the iron-on backing. Cut out the circles and stick them to the coloured fabric with an iron. Cut out the coloured circles, and then repeat with different colours of fabric.

2 Lay the bedlinen on a flat surface and work out where you want the circles to be – either in a pattern or randomly scattered. Peel off the paper backing and iron them into position.

⌛ 2 HOURS

You will need
- pencil
- circular object for drawing round
- iron-on backing
- scissors
- iron
- coloured fabrics
- plain bedlinen
- embroidery threads
- needle

3 Use a variety of different coloured embroidery threads to blanket stitch around the circles to finish.

Tie-dye bedlinen

It's easy to transform plain white sheets and pillowcases into something more eye-catching, and tie-dye is a fun technique to try at home. You can do it by hand or in the washing machine.

1 Dampen the sheet and lay it flat on the floor. Pinch the centre of the fabric and hold up the sheet from the centre point, letting the edges hang down. Tightly tie a length of string round the sheet 7.5cm (3in) from the centre point. Repeat at 7.5cm (3in) intervals until you reach the edges. Repeat with the pillowcases.

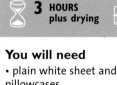

3 HOURS plus drying

You will need
- plain white sheet and pillowcases
- string
- scissors
- rubber gloves
- fabric dye
- measuring jug
- washing-up bowl or bucket
- salt
- dye fix

2 Wearing rubber gloves, dissolve the dye in hot water (check instructions for quantity) in the measuring jug, and pour into a bowl or bucket. Dissolve the salt and dye fix in hot water and add to the bucket. Check the manufacturer's instructions carefully in case they differ.

3 Immerse the bedlinen fully in the dye solution and leave for about an hour, again checking with the manufacturer's instructions.

4 Keeping the string in place, rinse the bedlinen in cold water until the water runs clear – you may be able to do this in your washing machine. Untie the string and wash the linen in hot water using a normal washing detergent, and leave to dry away from direct heat.

Shaker wallhanging

Use natural, country-style fabrics to give your bed an unusual, homely backdrop.

1 Cut the calico to the required size and decorate the edges with a border of red gingham. Fix the border in place using iron-on hem tape on the outer and inner edges of the border.

2 Use a tab-top kit to make strips from the gingham. Attach them to the top of the wall hanging. Cover the buttons from the tab-top kit with calico for a coordinated look.

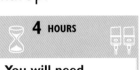

4 HOURS

You will need

- calico
- tape measure
- scissors
- red gingham
- pins
- iron-on hem tape
- tab-top curtain kit
- pencil or tailor's chalk
- pink gingham
- curtain pole
- screws
- drill
- wallplugs

3 Use a pencil or tailor's chalk to draw a heart on the pink gingham, and one on the red gingham fabric. Cut out the heart shapes, hem the edges carefully and place the hearts in the centre of the wallhanging. Once they are neatly positioned fix them to the centre of the wallhanging using iron-on hem tape.

4 Thread the tabs of the wallhanging on to the curtain pole and fix in position over the bed.

Eyelet blind

A blind that does not pull up is simple to make and provides an effective screen to block sunlight or an unpleasant view.

1 Measure the fabric to fit the window allowing 2cm (¾in) all round for hems. Cut out lining fabric to the same size.

2 Lay the fabric on a flat surface right side up and position the lining on it, right side down. Match all sides, pin and sew round all four sides, leaving a gap along part of the top seam.

3 Turn the blind right sides out and sew up the gap by hand. Press well.

4 Sew the eyelet tape along the back of the fabric on the underside of the blind and cut out the circle inside each eyelet using scissors. Use the clip-on rings to disguise and secure any rough edges.

5 Screw in the hooks along the top of the window frame and hook the eyelets on to them to hold the blind in place.

6 If you like this idea but wish to allow more light in, you could adapt the idea to unlined lace or voile.

⏳ **4 HOURS**

You will need:
- tape measure
- scissors
- fabric to cover the window area
- pins
- lining fabric
- iron
- eyelet tape
- eyelet kit
- sewing machine and cotton
- cup hooks

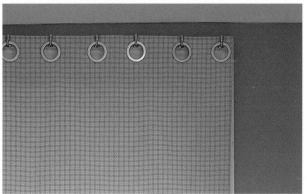

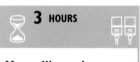
Padded headboard

Use a pretty pastel print to match or coordinate with your bedlinen to make this modern variation on a headboard.

1 Cut two pieces of fabric for the panels, each measuring 64x130cm (25x51in) for a standard double bed. Check the width of your bed to make sure this size suits.

2 Cut a long strip of fabric for the tap tops of the curtains, measuring 120x10cm (48x4in). Fold the strip in half lengthways with right sides facing and sew the two open edges together with a narrow seam.

⏳ **3 HOURS**

You will need
- patterned fabric
- scissors
- tape measure
- sewing machine or needle and cotton
- iron
- pins
- 2 foam pads, 2.5cm (1in) thick and 60cm (24in) square
- dowelling rod
- screws
- screwdriver
- hooks

Pull through the right way, press with an iron, and cut into eight 15cm (6in) lengths. Fold each in half.

3 Fold the panel pieces in half widthways, with right sides facing. Pin tabs along the top edge, equally spaced, with their raw edges aligned with the top of the fabric and the tabs themselves sandwiched between the two layers of fabric.

4 Sew along the top, fixing the tabs in place, down on one side and halfway down the other.

5 Turn right sides out, insert a piece of foam into each cover and sew up the gap. Thread the dowel through the tabs and attach the dowel to the wall with hooks.

Patchwork picture

There is something very satisfying about framing and hanging something you have created yourself. You don't have to be an artist to make this patchwork picture, and the fun is in choosing and arranging the fabrics.

1 Take time in deciding which fabrics to use and in what order – limiting yourself to pastel shades makes this easier as you are less likely to get unfortunate juxtapositions.

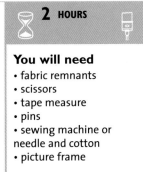

2 HOURS

You will need
- fabric remnants
- scissors
- tape measure
- pins
- sewing machine or needle and cotton
- picture frame

2 Cut 10cm (4in) squares from the fabric remnants. Pin then stitch them together in rows to roughly fit within the frame, then add strips of plain fabric to the outside edges and sew in place.

3 Stretch the fabric over the backboard of the picture frame and replace in the frame.

Dining in style

Special occasion cloth

Dress the table with a plain white cloth. Decorate it randomly with fresh, flat flower heads, leaving gaps for plates and serving bowls. Cut a piece of white organza to the same size as the tablecloth and place

⧖ 30 MINUTES

You will need
- white tablecloth
- fresh flowers
- scissors
- white organza fabric

over the table. For extra decoration complete with a vase of flowers.

As an alternative you could use artificial flowers but they need to be soft and flexible.

Flowery kitchen table

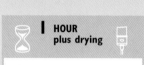

Sand the table legs and frame and paint with an oil-based paint; allow to dry.

Measure the table top and cut the piece of oil cloth to fit, adding an extra 15cm (6in) on all sides. Lay the oil cloth on top of the table and, pulling it tight as you go around, fold it over the

⧖ I HOUR
plus drying

You will need
- old wooden table
- sandpaper
- oil-based paint
- paintbrush
- tape measure
- patterned oil cloth
- scissors
- staple gun

edges and staple it to the underside of the table top. Make sure you fold in the corners neatly.

Napkin tie

Fold the napkin into a square and then roll up carefully. Cut a length of organza ribbon long enough to tie round the napkin, allowing for a bow and tail.

Cut a fresh flower stem about the same length as the rolled napkin. Place the stem either straight along the rolled napkin or arrange it diagonally and tie into position using the ribbon.

I0 MINUTES per napkin

You will need
- napkin
- organza ribbon
- scissors
- fresh flower

Beaded runner

Measure the table and cut a rectangle of fabric to size to make the runner, allowing extra for hems. The width should be about 40cm (16in) for most tables and the length should allow the runner to fall at either end, as in the picture. Use iron-on hem tape to hem all four sides.

2 HOURS

You will need
- tape measure
- fabric
- scissors
- iron-on hem tape
- iron
- pins
- beads
- needle and cotton

At each end, take the corners and fold inwards until they meet in the middle to form a point. Pin in place. Fix in place with iron-on hem tape. Sew on beads, equally spaced, around the edges of the runner.

Lace and ribbons

Coloured nets

Transform plain net or lace curtains by dyeing them. Wash the curtains and, while they are still damp, place them in a bowl of cold water dye for one hour, using a fixative with the dye

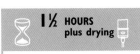

1½ HOURS
plus drying

You will need
• net or lace curtains
• cold water dye
• dye fix

and stirring every 20 minutes. Make sure you mix the dye and fixative well before immersing the curtains. Rinse, wash and dry the curtains.

Lace panel curtains

Wash, dry and press the lace panels. Lay one cotton curtain, right side up, on a flat surface. Put a lace panel on top, placing it centrally and aligning the top just below the tabs of the cotton curtain.

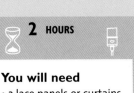

2 HOURS

You will need
• 2 lace panels or curtains
• iron
• plain cotton tab-top curtains
• needle and cotton
• scissors

Handstitch across the top of the lace panel to secure it to the curtain top. You may wish to make more than one row of stitches, but bear in mind you will have to unpick them each time you wash the curtains. Repeat with the other curtain.

Lace pelmet

Cut a piece of lace fabric one and a half times wider than the window and around 25cm (10in) deep. Dye the lace to tie in with your colour scheme.

2 HOURS
plus drying

You will need
- lace fabric
- scissors
- tape measure
- fabric dye (optional)
- peg rail
- primer
- wood paint

Fix a simple peg rail above the window, with one peg at either end and one in the middle. Prime, then paint it the same colour as the window frame. Leave to dry. Hang the length of lace from the pegs, to drape across the top of the window.

Lace table treatment

Make a side table look special by covering it with a lace cloth. This simple touch creates a delicate traditional look in an instant and can be used to disguise a less than perfect table surface.

10 MINUTES

You will need
- plain table cloth
- lace panel or curtain
- tape measure

Measure the top and a third of the drop of the table to give you an idea of the size of lace panel you need. If you can't find a panel to fit, use some lace curtain fabric which comes ready hemmed.

Blues and pinks

Blues and pinks blend together wonderfully for a classic pastel scheme. Introduce these pretty fondant shades through curtains, sheer fabrics, cushions, throws and decorative accessories.

▼ Transform a plain cushion with simple appliqué motifs in sparkly materials.

▲ Mix candy checks with flowers to give a more modern appeal to a scheme.

▲ Decorate a plain picture frame with strings of sparkly sequins.

▲ Hanging shelves make a modern alternative to open storage and are practical and inexpensive. Sheer fabrics in pastel colours look wonderful together.

▲ Mix baby blues and candy pinks with white bedlinen for a colourful, refreshing look.

▲ Make an old jumper into a novel cushion cover. Turn it inside out, cut off the sleeves, sew up the armholes, then stitch across the top. Turn right side out, insert a cushion pad and sew across the bottom.

Pastel combinations

Most pastel colours combine harmoniously together, and can be introduced into a scheme in a variety of ways. The trick is to team pastels of the same tone for a unified look. Alternatively, mix one shade with white for a simple, uncomplicated scheme.

▼ A row of pretty pastel bags hung on hooks makes a quick and inexpensive storage idea.

▲ A tablecloth makes an inexpensive window treatment. Simply attach to curtain clips and hang at the window.

▲ Soft pinks and lilacs make a wonderful colour combination and are perfect in subtle bedroom schemes.

▲ Combine cushions in sorbet pinks and soft blues for a pretty bedroom feel – they will work against almost all pastel backdrops.

▲ Checked voile panels make a clever and inexpensive makeshift wardrobe. Hang with curtain clips on a dowelling rod, suspended over a clothes rail.

▲ Pale pinks and greens work wonderfully together for a beautifully colour-schemed lounge. Accents of deep pink and plum bring them to life and provide contrasting tones.

Lavender hues

Lavender and subtle lilac shades create a calming and relaxing environment and combine beautifully with touches of blue, pink and silver. They are ideally suited in rooms used for relaxation, such as a bedroom or bathroom.

▼   Sew a length of beaded trim on to a panel of organza to make a lovely throw for your bed.

▲   Simple white plates and napkins look lovely with a dash of colour. Tie a pretty flower head to the centre of each napkin to make a charming table setting.

▲   Bundle a handful of dried lavender in a square of muslin or a handkerchief and tie with ribbon to hang over your taps for a relaxing bathtime treat.

▲ A single flower placed along a folded napkin and tied with a ribbon in a coordinating colour makes a pretty table decoration.

▲ Sew pockets on to an organza panel, edge with ribbon and fill with bunches of lavender to deter bugs – lavender is a natural insect repellent.

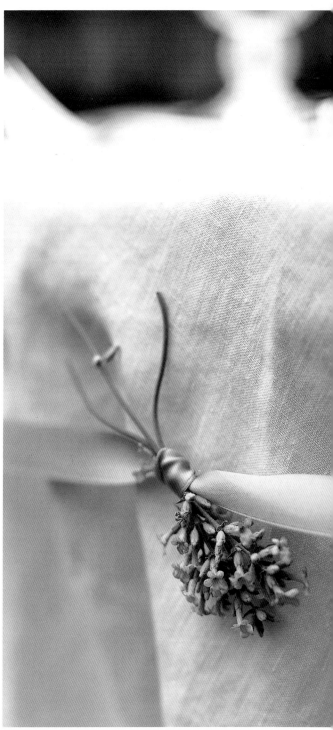

▲ Cover the table with a white tablecloth and cut enough ribbon to fit around the table, allowing a little extra for fastening. Tie the ribbon around the tablecloth, attaching a sprig of lavender at intervals.

Apple green with roses

Use soft, apple green as the basis for a calming, restful scheme with a summery feel.

Soft greens are restful and easy to live with, making them a popular choice for living rooms and bedrooms. Add interest with softly contoured furniture and patterned soft furnishings – unfussy treatments are often the most successful in a pastel room.

Introduce rose pink tones to complement the green. Plain weaves would look too structured in this romantic, room. Pretty floral prints add to the look without being too feminine. Use two coordinating florals to create a stronger impact. Contrast the fullness of pencil pleat curtains with a simple Roman blind – it's these details that give your room an individual touch.

Let the walls speak for themselves – there's no need to add lots of decorative finishes. The soft apple green reflects any natural light and still looks fresh in artificial light. A pale carpet works best as it keeps the room fresh and light. These peaceful pastel colours will make your home feel a more relaxing and tranquil place.

What else would work?

- painted floorboards
- natural-toned carpets
- pictures in pinky red tones

▲ Canvas panels painted with pale pastel shades create a focal point in the room and bring a more modern feel to the otherwise romantic, feminine look.

▲ Use flowers to accentuate this soft and fresh feel. Pinks give a lovely contrast.

▲ Beaded or sequinned cushions give textured prettiness.

Sylvia Edwards
• Noah's Place •

Bright kid's room

Use a mix of soft pinks and chalky blue with splashes of red to create a fun, stimulating bedroom for a young child.

The variety of colour and pattern on the bed make it the main focal point for the room. Choose simple floral bedlinen – this cheerful pink and white works perfectly on the decorative cream iron bed. A soft throw in red and white adds an extra cosy feel and provides a strong accent colour, echoed in the fun, tasselled lampshade.

A mid chalky blue paint really helps to bring the room to life and works wonderfully with pink. For a coordinating look, furniture has been given a coat of pink paint to pull the whole scheme together.

To keep a child's bedroom neat and tidy, storage is essential. Simple colourful plastic crates provide plenty of space for toys and can be stored neatly under the bed. Finish with soft cream accessories and hang large colourful pictures on the walls to add to the fun.

What else would work?

- lilac instead of pink
- plain wood bedhead
- white-painted wood bedhead
- colourful stripy bedlinen

▲ To keep a neat and orderly look, storage is a must. Plastic crates make a practical alternative to furniture – mix and match the colours for a stimulating effect.

▲ Red accessories add bold colour to the look. Use them as simple touches, such as a warm and cosy blanket.

▲ Plain and unexciting furniture can be given a funky new look with a coat of colourful paint.

Rich pastel bedroom

For a relaxing, dreamy environment, choose a palette of rich pastels.

For this dreamy bedroom scheme, steer clear of bold paint effects and go for plain walls or subtle details. Choose a soft aquamarine or turquoise, for an understated paint effect; add a subtle stripe of aqua along the top of the walls.

The bed is dressed with pretty pastels, and the be-ribboned pillows add decorative interest. Choose a few cushions with small floral detail for a light and pretty look. For a cosier feel, add throws in coordinating shades. Customize voile panels with lengths of coloured ribbon to create pretty ties. Ornate ironwork furniture looks lovely in this delicate scheme – opt for cream or white, giving existing pieces a lick of paint to pull the look together.

Painted wooden floors look fabulous with this look. Choose plain white and scatter some soft chenille rugs in pastel shades for a touch of warmth.

What else would work?

- wooden furniture with a white woodwash
- white painted wooden furniture
- soft blue or lilac carpet
- bedlinen with a small floral print

▲ Plain voile or muslin panels tied with pastel ribbons create a fresh, airy feel.

▲ Use accessories in colours that blend with your scheme. Here, fresh blues help to give the room its sense of coordination.

▲ For a simple treatment, sew ribbons across plain white pillowcases as a pretty detail.

Bold brights

Brightly coloured soft furnishings work best in contemporary settings and can help to make a bold statement. Alternatively, they can be used against a subtle backdrop to create a slightly more subdued look, with splashes of invigorating colour. Bright colours make a plain interior look sophisticated and interesting. Choose printed and plain fabrics, as well as textures such as velvets and satin. Brights often work well together when mixed with a combination of patterns. Plain blocks of colour combine well with coloured borders, stripes and patterns for a bold, coordinated look. Checks, stripes and geometric prints create a bright, modern interior.

Polka dot lampshade

Add a splash of colour to a room with this bold polka dot lampshade. For a jazzier version, you could choose a brightly coloured bobble trim in contrasting spots.

1 If you are revamping an old shade ensure it is clean and completely free of grease. Cover the surrounding work area with newspaper and stand the shade on top.

⧖ **1 HOUR** plus drying 🖌

You will need
- lampshade
- newspaper
- spray paint
- round white stickers
- strong glue
- bobble trim

2 Shake the spray can well. Before you spray the lampshade, practise spraying on the newspaper to perfect the technique. Hold the spray can 30–40cm (12–16in) from the shade while spraying and move the can from left to right until the surface is evenly covered. Take your time and remember that several light coats are better than one heavy one. Leave to dry.

3 Starting close to the top, stick white spots vertically on to the shade, leaving around 2.5cm (1in) between each sticker. Continue around the shade, spacing evenly.

4 Dab glue along the bottom rim of the shade and along the inside of the bobble trim. Working carefully, fix the bobble trim securely in place. Allow to dry thoroughly.

Decorative director's chair

Give an old director's chair a new lease of life by dressing
it with denim, sequins, beading and diamanté.

1 Remove the old covers and wash down the frame with a mild detergent to remove any excess dirt.

2 Once the frame is dry, sand the edges of the chair frame with medium grade sandpaper to give a weatherbeaten look.

3 Using the old chair covers as a pattern, cut new ones out of denim. Hem the edges neatly.

5 HOURS
plus drying

You will need:
- detergent and cloth
- sandpaper
- denim to cover the chair
- scissors
- sewing machine or needle and cotton
- stencil
- craft knife (if making own stencil)
- masking tape
- newspaper
- spray/fabric paint
- sequins
- diamanté beads
- beaded fringing

4 Either buy an alphabet stencil from a craft shop or make your own on a computer. Print the letters out and carefully cut out the letters with a craft knife. If you are using a ready made stencil, draw the word on a piece of paper first so you know how much room it takes up and can place it on the chair back.

5 Lay the chair back on a flat surface and attach the stencil with masking tape. Mask off adjacent areas with newspaper and ensure the surrounding area is well protected before spraying.

6 Apply several light coats, rather than one heavy one, until the letters are filled in. Alternatively, draw a freehand design using fabric pens or paints, following the manufacturer's instructions.

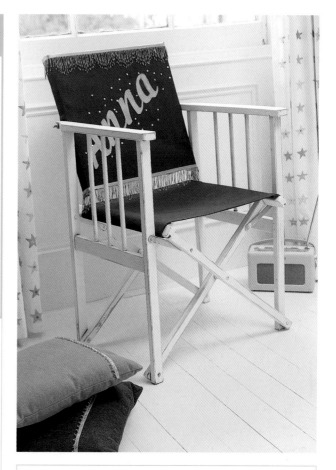

7 For the decoration, sew sequins and diamanté beads randomly around the design. Sew beaded fringing to the top and bottom of the chair back. Finally, slide the covers back on to the frame.

Room dividers

Separate a dual-purpose room with co-ordinating fabric banners for a chic, contemporary look.

1 Measure the height of the room. Cut out fabric panels that are the height of the room, plus another 12cm (5in) for hems, and as wide as you choose, allowing 7.5cm (3in) extra for side hems.

3 HOURS

You will need
- tape measure
- fabric
- scissors
- iron-on hem tape
- iron
- hacksaw
- 2 lengths of dowelling
- 2 screw-in hooks per panel

2 Make a 2cm (¾in) hem all round each panel using iron-on hem tape. On both long edges, fold over another 2cm (¾in) hem and secure again with hem tape. This will give neat edges on both sides.

3 At the top and bottom of each panel, fold over 6cm (2½in) and secure with hem tape to make a channel.

4 Use a hacksaw to cut a length of dowelling just shorter than the width of the panel and insert it into the bottom channel as a weight. Cut another piece 10cm (4in) longer than the width of the panel and slide it into the top channel.

5 Screw the hooks into the ceiling at a distance apart just wider than the panel. Hang the dowelling from the hooks.

Ribbon drapes

Create soft floaty panels for your windows and decorate with silky ribbons.

1 Measure the window. The fabric should drape in soft folds, so add 20–25 per cent to the width, and allow extra all round for the hems. Cut the organza according to your calculations.

2 HOURS

You will need
- tape measure
- organza fabric
- scissors
- pins
- sewing machine or needle and cotton
- ribbons

2 Turn a small hem on all sides of the organza panel. Pin, then sew in place.

3 Lay the panel flat on a work surface. Cut a selection of coloured ribbons to the width of the organza panel, allowing ½cm (³⁄₁₆in) to double under at each end.

4 Pin the ribbons across the curtain carefully, arranging them at different intervals until you have a pattern you are happy with. Stitch the ribbons in place. Make sure the ribbons sit as straight as possible across the fabric. Stitch the ribbons in place using a similar coloured cotton for each coloured ribbon.

4 Cut shorter lengths of ribbon for the ties, making sure they are all cut to the same length. Fold them in half so you have two equal lengths for each tie, then stitch them at equal distances along the top of the curtain. Tie the curtain to the pole with the ribbons.

Fuchsia pinks

Rosebud cushion

Take a plain silk cushion cover and lay it on a flat surface. Use tailor's chalk and a ruler to draw an even 7.5cm (3in) grid on the cover. Carefully sew the rosebuds on to the cushion where the lines cross.

2 HOURS

You will need
• silk cushion cover and cushion
• tailor's chalk
• ruler
• appliqué rosebuds
• needle and cotton

Simple pinboard

Draw four rectangles of the same size on to sheets of thick cardboard, then cut them out. Next cut out four fabric rectangles, each 5cm (2in) bigger all round than the pieces of cardboard. Cover the boards with the fabric, fastening at the back with tape.

Stick the boards to the wall using touch-and-close pads, checking they are straight with a spirit level.

30 MINUTES

You will need
• strong, thick cardboard
• pencil
• ruler
• scissors
• fabric or felt
• double-sided sticky tape
• self-adhesive touch-and-close pads
• spirit level

Decorative coasters

Cut out four pieces of card, 10x10cm (4x4in). Starting from the outside, measure a length of sequins to fit one edge. Glue down and repeat the process along the other edges to form a square.

Using squares of different coloured sequins, repeat this process until you reach the middle of the coaster.

Allow the glue to dry, then repeat with the other coasters. Tie neatly with a ribbon if you are giving them as a gift.

Roman blind

Cut fabric to fit the window, allowing an extra 2.5cm (1in) all round for hems. Use iron-on hem tape to fix the hems in place. Measure out the positions for the dowelling casings across the back of the blind, at 30cm (12in) intervals. Cut strips of fabric for the casings and pin, then sew them across the blind. Slide the dowelling into the casings.

Sew curtain rings evenly spaced and aligned to the bottom edge of each casing. Tie lengths of cord to the bottom ring in each row and thread up through the row of rings. Attach the blind to the window frame with upholstery tacks and screw in eyes to align with rings on blind. Feed cords through eyes and to one side, and hold together with a cord. Fix cleat to side of window frame to hold cords when blind is raised.

More curtain tricks

Layered curtains

Take two pieces of coloured muslin, each the width of the window and twice the length of the drop from the pole to the floor, then deduct 40cm (16in) from one of the lengths. Here the orange one is shorter.

| ⧖ | **1 HOUR** | 🖌 |

You will need
• pink muslin
• orange muslin
• tape measure
• scissors
• pins
• iron-on hem tape
• iron

Secure 2cm (¾in) hems with pins then attach iron-on hem tape all round each piece, with the top hems turned to the front of the fabric and bottom hems to the back. Lay the short piece out flat on the floor and lay the longer piece on top, lining up the bottom hems.

Drape both pieces over the curtain pole so the fabric hangs down in a double layer. Hold each curtain to the side with a matching tie-back.

Blanket curtain

Take the blanket and hang it over the curtain pole. You will need to pull the top edge over the front of the pole to create a fringed effect. Once you are happy with the proportions, and

| ⧖ | **15 MINUTES** | 🖌 |

You will need
• fringed blanket
• large curtain clips

the blanket is placed evenly, hold it in place with large curtain clips.

Tie-dye curtains

Dampen the curtains and lay them on a flat surface. Fold them lengthways into tight concertina pleats to form a thin strip. Bind tightly every 10cm (4in) with string or elastic bands.

I HOUR
plus drying

You will need
- plain cotton curtains
- string or elastic bands
- cold water dye
- cold water fix
- bucket
- wooden spoon
- plastic bag
- scissors

Prepare the dye and fix in the bucket, stir well with a wooden spoon and immerse the curtains in the dye for a few minutes. Lift the curtains out, place in a plastic bag, then tie the top tightly and leave overnight.

Remove the curtains from the bag and rinse them in cold water until the water runs clear (still with the ties attached). Remove the ties and wash them with a normal washing detergent. Allow to dry away from direct sunlight.

Daisy ribbon blind

Cut the broom handle or dowel to fit inside the window recess and prime, then paint it to match the frame. Cut the ribbon to the desired lengths. Round off one end with scissors, then pull the silk flower heads off their stalks and remove any bulky plastic pieces that might be attached.

Use strong glue to stick a flower to the rounded end of each ribbon. Attach a piece of double-sided sticky tape to the other end of the ribbon and stick to the back of the broom handle. Finally, fix the broom handle to the window frame with hooks.

I½ HOURS

You will need
- broom handle or thick dowel
- saw
- wood primer
- paintbrush
- oil-based paint
- ribbon
- scissors
- silk daisies
- strong glue
- double-sided sticky tape
- screw-in hooks

Exotic effects

Bangle tie-back

This decorative idea works best on coloured, lightweight curtains. An adjustable bangle with an opening offers the easiest way to make this tie-back. Hang the curtains and then bunch them together.

⏳ **10** MINUTES 🖌

You will need
• coloured lightweight curtains
• beaded adjustable bangle

At the middle point along the length of the curtain, fix the coloured bangle around the curtain to make a pretty, instant tie-back.

Glamorous bedlinen

Make a simple silk panel from decorative fabrics to complement your duvet cover. Cut a square paper template to the size you want the panel to be. Fold in half between two opposite corners to form a triangle and use to cut out two equal-sized triangles from your fabrics.

⏳ **1** HOUR 🖌🖌

You will need
• plain bedlinen
• scrap paper
• scissors
• Indian fabric remnants
• tailor's chalk
• pins
• needle and cotton
• iron

Use the template to mark out the position of the panel on the duvet cover using tailor's chalk, then pin the two triangles to the cover, turning the edges under. Stitch the traingles in place with a large running stitch around the outside and along the diagonal where the two fabrics meet. Press with an iron.

Make sure that the silk fabrics you use for the panel are machine washable.

Sari bedhead

Make a stunning focal point above your bed using a swathe of Indian sari fabric.

Fix a curtain pole from the ceiling with cup hooks. Cut a piece of sari fabric to twice the length of the drop and loop it over the pole. Catch the front section in a bangle tie-back.

30 MINUTES

You will need
- curtain pole
- 2 cup hooks
- drill
- screws
- screwdriver
- sari fabric
- scissors
- bangle or beaded wire

Velvet fringed cushion

Cut two squares of coloured velvet fabric the size of a cushion pad, allowing an extra 2cm (¾in) all round for hems. Place the two pieces of velvet together, right sides facing. Sew three sides together. Pin a zip to the fourth side and sew carefully in place.

I HOUR

You will need
- velvet fabric
- cushion pad
- tape measure
- scissors
- sewing machine or needle and cotton
- pins
- zip
- fringing

Cut four lengths of fringing the same length as the edges of the cushion. Carefully pin these to the front side of the cushion cover. Sew in place using a matching cotton, taking care to attach them to the front side of the cushion cover only.

A hint of luxury

Revamp and customize plain accessories with touches of sumptuous fabric. By simply adding a decorative border or panel a plain fabric can be transformed. Stockpile leftover pieces of fabrics and ribbons as they are ideal for these types of projects.

▼ Use luxurious cuts of sari fabric to make silky throws and cushions for the living room and bedroom to add a hint of eastern promise.

▲ Transfrom a tablecloth by turning it into napkins. Cut out and hem 25cm (10in) squares, roll up and tie with coloured ribbon to finish.

▲ Give an old chair a luxurious look by painting it and then covering it with a rich coloured velvet. Add cushions in contrasting colours.

▲ Give a plain lamp a jazzy touch by attaching a length of fluffy fur trim around the bottom of the shade.

▲ Use remnants of rich fabrics, such as Indian sari fabrics, to make pretty table mats, finishing with coloured cord or ribbon around the edges.

▲ Add panels of rich decorative fabrics to plain cushions to give a luxurious new look, using ribbon as a border.

Citrus shades

Vibrant citrus shades of yellow, orange and green work wonderfully together to create a bright and zingy look. You can really have fun with this scheme, and colours like lemon, tangerine and lime will lend an invigorating, sunny feel to any room. To cool the look down add touches of white.

▼   Mix bold prints, cushions of different textures and materials for a tactile finish to your room.

▲   Give plain throws a contrasting finishing touch by sewing a coloured zigzag stitch around the edges for a bright new look.

▲   Yellows, oranges and greens create a wonderful sunny feel – mix different fabrics together to add zing to the room.

▲ Boldly patterned bedlinen looks great with blocks of plain bright colour.

▲ A beaded lampshade adds a touch of glamour and it's also a great way to liven up dull colours.

▲ Mix different textures together for an interesting look. Combine velvet and textured cushions with waffle throws.

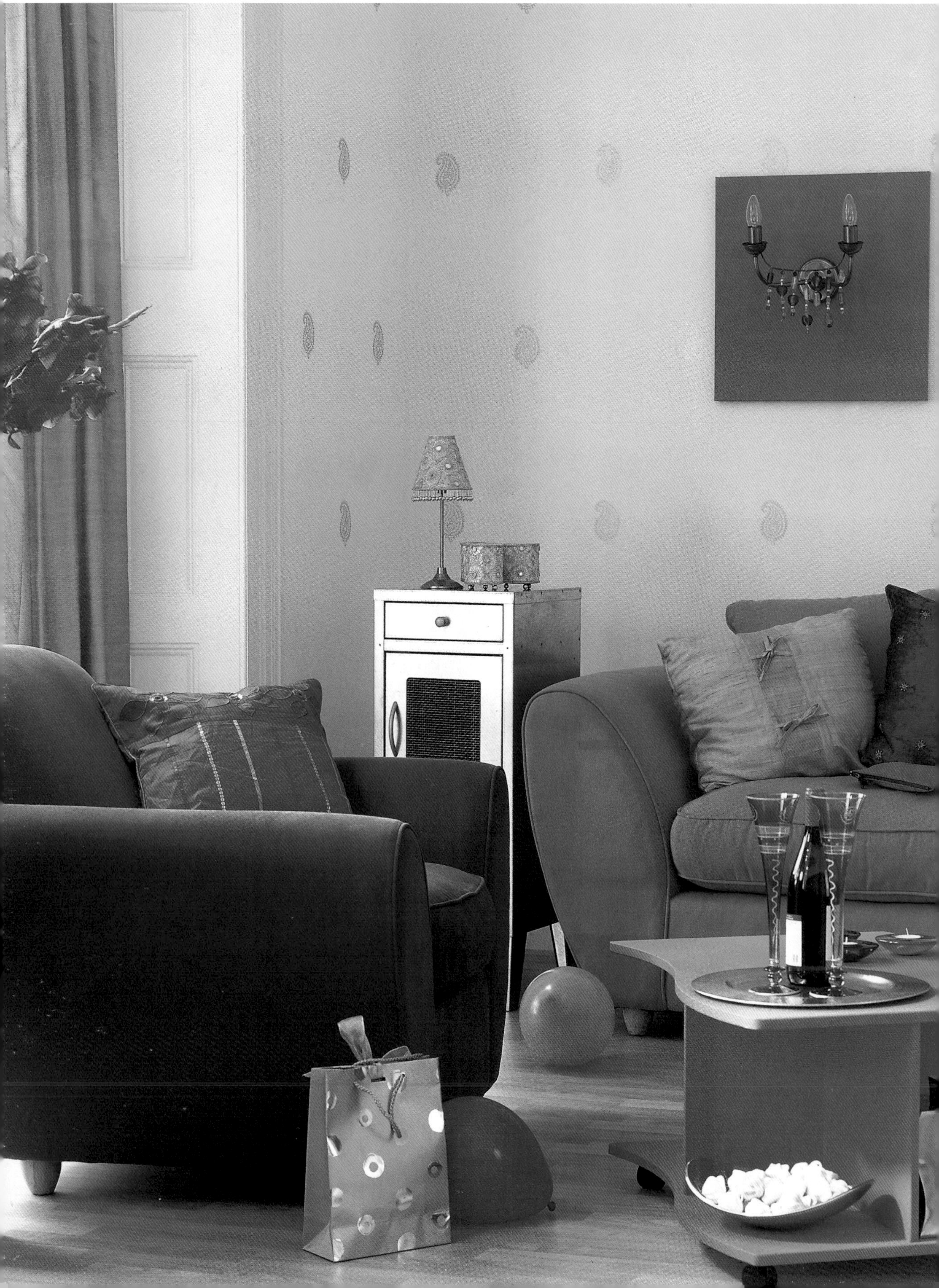

Eastern promise

Combine shimmering silks and beads in vibrant tones for a dazzling, exotic room.

In this vibrant and inviting scheme the white backdrop accentuates the luxuriant soft furnishings, giving the room a glamorous feel. A sofa and an armchair in bright blue shades look wonderful with contrasting cushions and throws.

Accessories and soft furnishings are the key to this look – choose shades of deep pink, lilac, purple and cobalt blue. Add fringing, embroidery, sequins and ribbons for an eye-catching effect. Use sari fabrics as throws, curtains or wall hangings for splashes of bold colour.

Here, furniture has been transformed to fit into the scheme with a lick of paint to coordinate with the fabrics. Walls have been given interest with a paisley design, using a stamp and silver paint. Finally decorative candelabras and chandeliers will give an added feel of glamour to the whole look.

What else would work?

- silvery blue soft pile carpet
- lilacs, blues and aqua greens
- velvet sofas

▲ For bold style, paint your furniture in bright pinks or lilac shades.

▲ Decorative beaded and embroidered cushions provide pattern while lifting the sofas and adding glitz to the general scheme.

▲ Add colour to the floor with big cosy floor cushions made from silk.

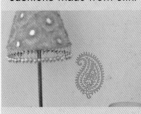

▲ A decorative stamp motif in silver paint gives an individual touch to the walls.

Oriental retreat

Add bold colour and Oriental prints to your living room with splashes of deep red.

The Oriental look is simplicity itself. Start off with a neutral backdrop, add a few designer tricks and the Oriental style is yours.

Black and red panels painted on to the wall create a strong theme but don't overwhelm the room. If paint seems too bold, try filling the panels with Oriental-themed wallpaper, with a calligraphy design, perhaps. A simple box-shaped sofa in rattan works perfectly here but has been enlivened with linen cushions with Oriental panels.

An authentic-looking screen would really add to this look. You could make one from MDF and paint a design on to it using a motif from the fabric or wallpaper, or alternatively use a motif fabric which coordinates with the other soft furnishings.

Keep flooring natural – a wooden floor or natural floor covering such as sisal looks great. If you want to go the whole hog, stain your furniture with a dark wood stain. Finally, add simple decoration in the form of lacquered bowls and a few orchids.

What else would work?

- plain box-style upholstered sofa
- natural materials such as linen and hessian
- textured carpet or floorcovering

▲ Add interest to plain cushions with simple stitched fabric panels that coordinate with the cushion cover.

▲ Look for wallpapers or fabrics with Oriental motifs or calligraphy and use lengths for screens, wall hangings or panels.

▲ The Oriental look relies on simple accessories, so don't overcrowd surfaces. Stick to simple bowls and architectural plants such as orchids.

Modern country

Mix bright, sunny yellows, white furniture and summery prints for an updated country look.

This sunny and colourful room looks great with white accessories for a lovely fresh feel. As everything else is fairly plain, a stripy sofa in a mix of yellow, white and green adds definition to the scheme, creating a strong focal point. A plain yellow throw adds a splash of simple colour, while cushions in stripes, plains and floral patterns add softness to the overall theme. To perfect the look, mix and match solid colours with textured plains, such as ribbed and waffle throws and cheerful striped fabrics.

Walls are painted in a fairly strong yellow to give a colourful backdrop; they are kept plain for a slightly more modern twist. A delicate, white voile panel at the window is ideal to enhance this fresh, airy feel, providing more brightness and light to the scheme. White armchairs provide blocks of colour to coordinate with the sofa. Painted white furniture adds crispness to the look, while a cherry wood laminate floor, finished with a simple white rug, brings a cosy warmth to the whole scheme.

What else would work?

- softer yellow walls
- light wood furniture
- neutral carpet

▲ Stripes add interest and a strong focal point as there is little pattern elsewhere.

▲ Introduce floral fabrics on to cushions and soft furnishings to enhance the country feel.

▲ To lift the room, add touches of pink, including a vase of tulips, to provide a pretty contrast to the room. A few pink accessories dotted around the room would also add a subtle contrast.

Bold bedroom

Create a cool, funky environment that focuses on colour and bold shapes – this look is perfectly suited to kids or teenagers, but can be adapted to all age groups.

Here, vivid pink bedlinen really adds a zing. To give the room a fun, cosy feel, add a bright rug and plenty of coloured cushions in greens and aquas. Paint the walls in aqua and bright green; you may want to confine these colours to just one or two walls, depending on the effect you want to achieve. Use stencil paint to create spots in pastel colours, such as pink, sorbet green and aqua. An easy way to achieve this effect is by dipping the end of a small roller in paint and dabbing it on the wall.

Keep furniture quite simple. Go for cheerful plastic storage on wheels and funky shaped plastic or resin seating in bright colours. A covered foam cube makes a great seat and beanbags can be piled up when they are not in use. A pink paper lantern adds simple and inexpensive decoration to the walls, while a piece of MDF has been painted with bright stripes and hung up as a picture.

What else would work?

- Beech furniture
- just one colour on the walls
- a simple border instead of spots

▲ Cushion covers like these can be made from fabric remnants, and they don't have to cost you a fortune.

▲ Plastic storage is particularly good for kids' rooms as it is colourful and indestructible.

▲ Polka dots add a fun feel to the room. If you don't want to use them on the walls, use them on soft furnishings instead.

Ethnic adventure

Take inspiration from the jewel colours of India, and spice up your home with a taste of the exotic.

This exotic scheme relies on a combination of rich, bold colours. A carved wooden bench makes a decorative alternative to a standard sofa and you can really go to town here with soft furnishings. Fill the room with plenty of silk cushions in spicy oranges, hot pinks and bright blues, with touches of gold decoration. Look out for sequins, beading and fringing to enhance the exotic feel. Saris and Indian embroidered fabrics are ideal in this room and can even be used as wallhangings.

Choose colourful decorative voiles for the windows, with embroidered patterns, or, alternatively, use sari fabric to create a simple panel curtain. Here the walls have been painted in a rich, turquoise shade to coordinate with soft furnishings. Continue the Indian theme with chunky dark wood furniture and finish with decorative gold or silver accessories.

What else would work?

- dark stained floorboards
- plain walls with just a decorative border or panel
- smaller pieces of decorative furniture

▲ Look out for unusual Indian fabrics in markets and haberdasheries, and use them to make throws and wallhangings to add real character to this scheme.

▲ Dark, carved wooden furniture really helps to give the room its definition.

▲ Have fun with soft furnishings; this is what this look is all about. Scatter lots of cushions in colourful shades on floors, chairs and sofas.

Index

Acknowledgements

All pictures are copyright of The National Magazine Company Limited.

Editor: Abi Rowsell
Executive Art Editor: Leigh Jones
Designer: Claire Harvey
Picture Researcher: Zoë Holtermann
Your Home **Picture Coordination:** Jill Morgan
Production Controller: Lucy Woodhead